WORD
BIBLICAL
THEMES

WORD
BIBLICAL
THEMES

Psalms

LESLIE C. ALLEN

WORD BOOKS
PUBLISHER
WACO, TEXAS

A DIVISION OF
WORD, INCORPORATED

PSALMS
Word Biblical Themes

Library of Congress Cataloging-in-Publication Data

Allen, Leslie C.
  The Psalms.

  (Word Biblical themes)
  Bibliography: p.
  Includes index.
  1. Bible. O.T. Psalms—Criticism, interpretation,
etc. I. Title. II. Series.
BS1430.2.A335   1987   223'.206   87-8184
ISBN 0-8499-0600-X   pap. 0-8499-3082-0

Printed in the United States of America
7898 RRD 987654321

To Joy

CONTENTS

FOREWORD

Everyone has favorite Psalms. Yet the book of Psalms is still a closed treasure to most of us. So many of them do not obviously speak to us in our deepest need.

This is a book that can help to open that treasure and make it possible for the reader to claim many more of them as personally relevant. It explains in language all can understand the way the Psalms have been collected and arranged and leads the reader through the different kinds of psalms before showing how they were used in different settings. These hymns and poems have proved to be remarkably adaptable to changing forms of worship through the centuries, yet, in all these changing forms, the Psalms keep the worshipers' attention focused on basic themes of God's goodness. These consist in emphasis on God's blessing and on his salvation. The Psalms then lead the worshiper to cultivate responses in praise, faith, and hope.

Like the teacher described in Matthew, who "brings out of his storeroom new treasures as well as old," Leslie Allen here provides for the reader a spiritual feast, the fruits of his study of Psalms in their original tongue. The reader who wishes to go more deeply into the foundations of what is written here will want to see the volume on Psalms 101–150 (No. 21) by Leslie Allen in the *Word Biblical Commentary*.

Dr. Allen's insightful book recognizes that the Psalms speak to each of us differently. Each reader comes to this book from a different perspective, yet the Psalms have prayers and songs for each of us.

Southern Baptist Theological
Seminary
Louisville, Kentucky

John D. W. Watts
Old Testament Editor
Word Biblical Commentary

1 INTRODUCTION

Of all the Old Testament books Psalms has a special place in the hearts of Christians. Such is its popularity that it is easy to purchase a copy of the combined New Testament and Psalms. Every believer has a list of favorite psalms, while probably paying little attention to the rest. Little oases of familiarity punctuate a desert of unfamiliarity. The very format of the Psalter lends encouragement to this tendency. The individual psalms do not function as chapters in a book. Their consecutive numbering carries no warranty of consecutive content. Many of the psalms have their own titles, which increases a sense of beginning afresh with each new number. As a result readers feel little inducement to get inside the world of the Psalms.

People commonly attach a label to the Psalter, calling it "the hymnbook of the Second Temple." This has some claim to truth, but on reflection it serves to accentuate the formlessness of the collection. Hymnbooks, as we know them, are arranged thematically according to particular doctrines and to periods in the church calendar. In no way do the psalms follow such an orderly pattern! A rare exception is the run of psalms celebrating God's kingship, Pss 96–99. Even here it is noticeable that the affiliated Ps 93 is separate from its fellows.

Are there any unifying principles behind the overall collection? Indeed there do appear to be, but it is good to appreciate its relatively random nature. There is a danger in trying to systematize the Psalms, the danger of wanting to find links that were never really there. The appearance of randomness is a witness to the gradual accumulative nature of this book. Here are centuries of devotion crammed into one book. In this respect the Psalter is a microcosm of the Bible as a whole. It is a rich heritage to which many generations have contributed through all the changing scenes of human history, and so generation after generation can take it to their hearts, feeling kinship with its pages. Nowhere is the scriptural interweaving of divinity and humanity more evident than here.

Before we can tackle the themes of the Psalms, there is a certain amount of background information for the reader to grasp. We need to find our way into and around the Psalter, so that we evaluate its contents aright.

Compilation

There is more than one way of analyzing the Psalms. Perhaps the best approach to begin with is to look at the end of the process which resulted in the canonical collection, and to discern the final editorial shape that has been imposed upon it.

1. *The five "books."* There is a consciousness that the hundred and fifty psalms comprise an anthology, a literary whole. Evidence of this consciousness lies in the fact that the overall collection has been divided into five sections or "books." The rabbis saw a parallel here with the Pentateuch,

the five books of Moses, as if the Psalter was planned as a counterpart, the five books of David. It is a plausible suggestion, but scholarly attempts to verify it, for instance by envisaging lectionary parallels between pentateuchal passages and the Psalms, have not won general acceptance. Each of the "books" has been given its own conclusion in the form of a doxology. Book One consists of Pss 1-41 and ends with Ps 41:13:

Blessed be the Lord the God of Israel from everlasting and
to everlasting!
Amen and Amen.

Books Two, Three, and Four end similarly, at 72:18, 19; 89:52 and 106:48, thus marking their dimensions as Pss 42–72, 73-89, and 90-106. Ps 106:48 shows that "Amen (and Amen)" was modeled on a congregational response to a call of praise, in affirmation and involvement:

Blessed be Israel's God Yahweh
from everlasting to everlasting,
and let all the people say "Amen."

These doxologies did not originally belong to the individual psalms among which they are numbered, but are related to the preceding section of psalms as a literary finale, an ovation in God's honor.

Book Five, Pss 107-150, does not have a doxology of the same type. It is generally thought that its last psalm, Ps 150, has the function of a doxology for both Book Five and the whole Psalter. In this series of asides which punctuate the collection we hear literary tributes of praise, in reaction to the portrayal of God given within each of its sections.

2. *The individual collections.* This scheme of books and doxologies is a final arrangement superimposed upon a large

Introduction

amount of earlier editorial work. The Psalter has grown by the accumulation of separate collections. It is like a well-loved hymnbook which over the years has gone through a number of editions, gradually enlarging its scope.

The primary collections which were utilized to build up the book of Psalms as we know it may be detected from the headings to individual psalms. Two collections represent the repertoire of Levitical choirs in the temple. Pss 42–49, 84, 85, and 87, 88 name "the sons of Korah" in their headings, while Pss 50, 73–83 are ascribed to "Asaph." Another group of psalms mentions not their singers but apparently the scene in which they functioned: the "Songs of Ascents," Pss 120–134. These were probably processional songs, sung as choirs and congregation "went up" through Jerusalem to the temple in sacred procession at festival time. Here then is evidence of a system of worship in which these psalms once played a role. They were meant to be sung and heard within a worshiping community whose hearts were in tune with the words of faith and praise.

Another collection may be detected from the *content* of its psalms. In certain psalms the content highlights the person of the Davidic king. Now scattered throughout the Psalter, originally they were probably a single collection. These royal psalms include Pss 2, 45, 101, 110, and 132. The society in which these psalms were first used did not have a constitution that demarcated religion from politics. It idealized a particular form of monarchy as the potential sphere of God's will and gave it a role in its official religion.

The backbone of the first half of the Psalter is made up of two collections associated with the name of David, Pss 3–41 and 51–71. We are uncertain to what extent the Davidic ascription was originally intended to refer to authorship of each of the psalms within the collection. There can be no objection in principle to the view that David composed psalms, in the light of the traditions elsewhere in the Old

Testament that associate him with music and poetry. Certain of the "Davidic" psalms, however, exhibit late features and would sound strange on David's lips. It may be that very early cores of the Davidic collections were gradually supplemented. Anyway, there eventually grew up a belief that credited David with authorship of all the Davidic psalms, a belief that is reflected in the colophon at 72:20, "The prayers of David, the son of Jesse, are ended." This trend continued into later times, so that the Greek version of the Psalter and Hebrew manuscripts found at Qumran variously increase the number of Davidic ascriptions.

In the New Testament Ps 2 is credited to David, at Acts 4:25; so too is Ps 95 in Heb 4:7, following the Greek version. Eventually the Psalter was considered "the treasury of David," to use the famous title of Spurgeon's commentary. Certain of the Davidic psalms have narrative headings which associate the compositions with particular events in David's life. They probably reflect later interpretation in most cases. They and the Davidic ascriptions in general reveal a perspective of the Psalter which will merit close attention in a later chapter.

3. *Editorial arrangement.* The Psalms are not simply a stringing together of various collections. Gerald H. Wilson has drawn attention to evidence of deliberate arrangement behind compilation of the Psalter.[1] The second group of Korahite psalms are Pss 84, 85, 87, and 88. Is there any evidence to suggest that Ps 86 has been deliberately inserted? A perusal of Pss 85–87 does indicate an overlap of theological content. Ps 85 and Ps 86 both celebrate in their early parts the forgiveness and steadfast love of God (85:2,7; 86:5) and in their latter portions his steadfast love and faithfulness (85:10; 86:15). Similarly, Pss 86 and 87 both affirm a conviction that God is to be worshiped by nations other than Israel (86:9; 87:4–6). So Ps 86 has been dovetailed into its Korahite neighbors in order to highlight their theological themes.

The nameless Ps 33 has been incorporated into a series of Davidic psalms, apparently in order to accentuate the content of 32:10,11:

The one who trusts in the Lord—
lovingkindness shall surround him!
Rejoice in the Lord and exult, you righteous ones. . . .

As in the former case, steadfast love or "lovingkindness" is hailed as a key attribute of God (32:10; 33:5, 18, 22), an attribute that is worthy of "rejoicing" on the lips of the "righteous" or "upright" congregation (32:11; 33:1). The message of this editorial arrangement is that God's gracious character should ever draw forth a response of praise.

Why is the Asaphite Ps 50 separate from its fellows in Pss 73–83? It seems to function as a bridge between the Korahite and Davidic collections (Pss 42–49; 51–71) because it shares adjacent concerns. Ps 50 begins with a description of Zion as a setting for God's revealing of himself in judgment, in seeming echo of 48:1–3. It includes a discussion of the role of sacrifice (50:8–15, 23) which is matched by the concern of 51:16–19. So Ps 50 serves to ease the linking of the two separate collections and, in the process, to stimulate theological thinking.

These examples of editorial ordering show a thoughtful interest in the thematic linking of particular psalms. In our own aim to group the material of the Psalter under themes we will not be engaging in any alien task. More remains to be said in later chapters about the impact of the completed Psalter upon the observant reader. Enough has been said, however, to reveal a lengthy architectural process of amassing blocks of material and building them together into larger wholes and eventually into an overarching unity. The book of Psalms is like an old English manor house built over the centuries in different styles, Tudor, Jacobean, and Georgian, each of whose later architects has labored with appreciation of the work of his predecessors, and has added his own distinctive contribution with sensitivity.

Types of psalms

Another way of getting inside the Psalter is to take a cross-section of it and examine the various kinds of psalms within it. It is obvious to everybody that Ps 3 is quite different from Ps 2. The differences between psalms were put on a scholarly basis by Hermann Gunkel in the first three decades of this century and by Sigmund Mowinckel, and their work has been developed especially by Hans-Joachim Kraus and Claus Westermann.[2] The academic approach to the Psalter is founded upon this perspective, which bears the name of form criticism.

A brief sketch of the results will be given here. It has proved of inestimable help in finding one's way through a veritable storeroom of literary objects left higgledy-piggledy. Form criticism has been concerned to identify and group similar psalms and to analyze the patterns of characteristic elements found in the resultant groups. The overall approach is a good servant but a bad master. It performs the valuable service of comparing scripture with scripture in such a way as to categorize psalms and to discern the standard elements of expression used in each group of psalms. In the process, however, there is a danger of blurring the individuality of particular psalms as they are judged in the light of hypothetical, generalized ideals.

1. *The individual lament.* This is the type most represented in the Psalter and predominant in the Davidic collections. Roughly a third of the Psalter belongs to this category. It is a poignant prayer wrung from personal crisis, such as severe sickness or social victimization, from which the sufferer seeks to be set free. There is a basic structure which

examples of this type tend to exhibit to a greater or lesser degree: (1) an initial petition explicitly addressed to God, (2) a stylized description of the crisis, (3) an affirmation of trust in God, (4) a main section of petition and (5) a vow of praise, once the prayer has been answered. A specimen of the individual lament that exemplifies these elements is Ps 56:

(1) Be gracious to me, O God, (v 1a)
(2) for men trample upon me;
    all day long foemen oppress me;
    my enemies trample upon me all day long
    for many fight against me proudly. (vv 1b, 2)
    All day long they seek to injure my cause;
    all their thoughts are against me for evil.
    They band together, they lurk,
    they watch my steps. (vv 5, 6a)
(3) When I am afraid,
    I put my trust in thee.
    In God, whose word I praise,
    in God I trust without a fear.
    What can flesh do to me? (vv 3,4)
    Thou hast kept count of my tossings;
    put thou my tears in thy bottle!
    Are they not in thy book? . . .
    Then my enemies will be turned back
    in the day when I call.
    This I know, that God is for me.
    In God, whose word I praise . . . ,
    in God I trust without a fear.
    What can man do to me? (vv 8–11)
(4) As they have waited for my life,
    so recompense them for their crime;
    in wrath cast down the peoples, O God! (vv 6b, 7)
(5) My vows to thee I must perform, O God;
    I will render thank offerings to thee.

For thou hast [or: wilt have] delivered my soul from death,
yea, my feet from falling
that I may walk before God
in the light of life. (vv 12, 13)

The fourth element is frequently longer, notably in 89:13–18, 22–28. The second element is often quite complex, with a threefold perspective: (a) what my enemies have done to me, (b) what I am suffering, and (c) what God has done to me. Ps 102 is an example of this comprehensive complaint, which relates to society, self, and God:

(a) All day long my enemies insult me,
    they use my name as a curse, ridiculing me. (v 8)
(b) My life is vanishing in smoke;
    my bones burn like embers . . .
    I lie awake and am
    like a solitary bird on a rooftop. (vv 3–7)
    Ashes I eat for my food. (v 9a)
    My life is like a lengthening shadow.
    I am shriveled up like grass. (v 11)
(c) With my drink I mingle tears
    because of your anger and your wrath;
    you have picked me up and thrown me away. (vv 9b, 10)
    He has brought low my strength part way through my
      course,
    he has decreed a short life for me. (v 23)

2. *The communal lament.* This is the collective counterpart to the individual lament. The communal lament responds to national crisis. It is represented much more sparingly in the Psalter: examples are Pss 44, 74, and 79. It has a similar structure, with addition of two extra elements, slipped into the second and penultimate positions respectively: a reference to God's work of salvation in the past and

a double wish or petition concerning the people and their enemies. Ps 79 is a good instance to look up and study in terms of its various parts.

These are the standard ways in which prayer in response to dire need is expressed in the book of Psalms, whether voiced by individuals or on behalf of the people of God. This praying is marked by realism and frank speaking: faith and pain are here an explosive combination of human chemicals. It is characterized by logical structuring, with the evident intent of persuading God to intervene by means of impressive arguments. One of the elements of lament, the affirmation of trust, may be expanded into a complete composition. Ps 23, everybody's favorite psalm, belongs to this category. Other instances are the individual Pss 4, 16, and 131, and the communal Ps 129.

3. *The song of thanksgiving.* Not surprisingly the "please" factor of the Psalter finds a sequel in a "thank you." The vow of praise which closes the lament hints as much. The thanksgiving song, which represents a fulfilling of the vow, logically follows the lament as the eventual expression of gratitude for answer to specific prayer. Examples of such individual songs are Pss 18, 30, 116, and 138. Strictly there appears to have been no distinctive form of communal thanksgiving, but the individual form could be adapted to fill this lack: Ps 124 is a rare instance.

The six elements common to most thanksgiving songs are: (1) and (2) a resolve to sing, with an introductory summary of release from crisis, (3) a description of the crisis, (4) a report that God has heard the prayer of lament and acted affirmatively, (5) generalized teaching, and (6) renewed thanksgiving. Ps 30 is a clear model of this type:

(1)&(2) I will extol you, O Lord, for you have drawn me out
         and have not allowed my enemies to rejoice over
         me.

O Lord my God, I called for help and you healed
me;
O Lord, you brought my soul up from Sheol:
from those going down to the Pit you made me
live. (vv 1–3)

(3) But I!—I said in my security:
"I will never be moved!"
O Lord, in your favor you made me stand more
erect than mountains of strength.
You hid your face—I was dismayed. (vv 6, 7)

(4) [I said:] "To you, O Lord, will I cry!
And to you, my Governor, will I plead for
mercy . . .
Hear, O Lord, and be merciful to me.
O Lord, be my helper."
You have changed my wailing to dancing for me;
you have removed my sackcloth and girded me
with rejoicing. (vv 8–11)

(5) Sing praises to the Lord, O you saints of his,
and praise his holy name.
For in his anger is death,
but in his favor is life.
Weeping may tarry in the evening,
but joy comes at dawn. (vv 4, 5)

(6) so that my soul shall sing your praise and not weep,
O Lord my God, I will praise you forever. (v 12)

4. *The hymn.* This is another key category, distinct from
the previous pair. The term *hymn* has a narrower sense than
in Christian usage. Like the song of thanksgiving it majors in
praise. The difference is that the thanksgiving song is crisis-
oriented along with the lament. It is a response to what God
has just done in the experience of the believing person or
community. The thanksgiving song is the religious equivalent of a burst of applause immediately after a performance

at the theater or concert hall. The hymn, on the other hand, lacks such immediacy. It surveys the character and work of God in a general fashion and from further afield.

If, as the final psalm asserts, it is the obligation of "everything that breathes" to "praise Yahweh" (150:6), it is hardly surprising that the hymn developed with a variety of forms. The simplest kind is that exhibited in the shortest psalm, Ps 117, which has two elements, (1) an imperative call to praise in v 1 and (2) the reason for praising in v 2:

> (1) Praise Yahweh, all nations,
>   laud him, all you peoples,
> (2) because his loyal love has towered over us
>   and Yahweh's faithfulness is everlasting.

This basic pattern is followed in longer hymns, such as Pss 113 and 146 and in solo adaptations, Pss 103 and 104. Other hymns double this pattern by repeating the pair of elements, such as Pss 100 (vv 1-2, 3-4, 5); 147 and 148. Themes of the hymn are God's roles in creation and in human history, and his dynamic attributes of steadfast love and power. A hymn may take a number of themes in its stride, like Pss 33 and 136. Or it may specialize, like Pss 103 (steadfast love), 104 (creation), and 105 (history).

There are subgroups of hymns, such as the psalms of divine kingship mentioned earlier. The Songs of Zion, notably Pss 46, 48, 76, and 87 praise God as the Lord of Jerusalem and of temple worship. A number of the royal psalms, particularly Pss 2, 21, 72, and 110, in focusing upon the Davidic king, were meant to honor God as Lord of the Davidic covenant. The term "royal psalm" is not strictly a form-critical category: it can take the form of a lament (Ps 89) or a song of thanksgiving (Pss 18, 118).

There are also smaller groupings of psalms, such as the

wisdom psalms and prophetic and priestly liturgies, which need not be mentioned in the present survey. Enough has been said to indicate the general range of expression covered in the pages of the Psalter. The religious contexts in which this range was evidently used and its relation to the gamut of human experience will be the topics of the next chapter.

2 FUNCTION

For Christians today the Psalter has a variety of uses. In a church setting a psalm may be employed as a scripture reading before a sermon based upon it. In certain denominations the Psalter is used as a lectionary; antiphonal recitation or chanting of set psalms makes a rich contribution to the worship and prayer of the service. The psalms have also been paraphrased for the congregation to sing as hymns. In quite a different setting, the Psalter is read and studied by individual Christians as an aid to personal devotion. In motel rooms travelers find a Gideon Bible which in its preface urges them to turn to Ps 23 for help in time of need, to Ps 19 for the doctrine of the twofold revelation of God and to Ps 15 for business and professional principles.

What of the Psalter in its Old Testament context? The answers to this question are not immediately obvious. The Psalms are a medley of voices calling in the dark, and we can no longer see plainly where the owners of these disembodied voices are or what they are doing. Perhaps we do not need to peer and our question is improper curiosity. Yet there are clues inside and outside the Psalter which help to clarify the different backgrounds behind the Psalms and which can enrich our understanding of them.

Temple settings

Sigmund Mowinckel urged that most of the psalms were composed for use in a temple setting,[3] and the majority of subsequent scholars have followed his lead in general, if not in his particular reconstructions.

1. *The communal lament.* The habitat of the communal lament seems not unnaturally to have been the national sanctuary. Solomon's prayer associated with the dedication of the temple in 1 Kgs 8 supports a setting in the courts facing the temple:

> When thy people are defeated before the enemy . . . , if they . . . pray and make supplication to thee in this house, then hear thou in heaven. . . . When heaven is shut up and there is no rain . . . , if they pray to- ward this place . . . , then hear thou in heaven . . .
> (vv 33–36)

So do the exhortations of Joel in reaction to a severe plague of locusts that threatened the very existence of the Judean community. There is mention of the convening of a national assembly in the temple area and of priestly utterance of a communal lament (Joel 1:13, 14; 2:15–17). Similarly, 2 Chr 20 gives details of a national convocation in the temple court and the king's voicing of such a lament (vv 4–12).

Both 2 Chr 20 and Joel go on to relate a divine response in the form of a prophetic oracle, a phenomenon that finds a parallel in Ps 85. This psalm is a prophetic liturgy, a composi- tion in which two sets of voices are heard, one of which is that of a temple prophet. The first half, vv 1–7, is a communal lament, while a solo voice breaks into the second half, vv 8–15, transmitting God's reply:

> Let me hear what God the Lord will speak.
> He speaks peace to his people, . . . (v 8)
> [RSV does not express what needs to, and may, be said]

In this case the answer consists of a single word, "peace," *shalom* in Hebrew. It spells reconciliation to God and the renewal of good relations, and so an end to the wrath evident in the national crisis, mentioned earlier in the psalm. Verses 9–13 are a prophetic exposition of the reply, equating this *shalom* with the "steadfast love" and "salvation" for which the people had asked in v 7:

> Surely his salvation is at hand for those that fear him . . .
> Steadfast love and faithfulness will meet;
> righteousness and peace will kiss each other. . . .

Ps 60 envisages a similar situation: the oracle spoken by God "in his sanctuary" (vv 6–8) follows the communal lament of vv 1–5. One may look up and compare the divine oracle of 12:5.

2. *The individual lament.* Similarly the lament of the individual had its natural habitat at the sanctuary. The poignant narrative of the childless Hannah pouring out her heart at the sanctuary of Shiloh and the blundering priest who at last understands her state of mind and gives her his blessing (1 Sam 1:9–18), adds human flesh and blood to the anguished voices that ring out in the Psalter. So does the story of Hezekiah's resorting to the Jerusalem temple and dramatically spreading out in Yahweh's presence the intimidating letter from the Assyrian emperor (2 Kgs 19:1, 14–19). These narratives suggest that when the heading to Ps 102 defines the following lament as "a prayer for a sufferer when he feels

Function

weak and pours out his worries before Yahweh," the final phrase refers to the ark housed in the temple, which was regarded as the token of God's presence.

The person who recited his or her lament or had it recited hoped for an affirmative word from God. Lam 3:55–57 appears to testify to such a phenomenon as a previous experience, while hoping for a fresh answer to prayer: the divine word in that case was "do not fear." The reassurance is akin to Eli's response "go in peace" in 1 Sam 1:17. Within the Psalms themselves there is evidence that is best interpreted as pointing to divine intervention through a priest or prophet. Such intervention seems to underlie statements in certain individual laments that God has heard the prayer, such as 6:8–10 and 28:6. Ps 28:5 represents a prophetic assurance about the psalmist's foes:

> Because they do not understand the works of the Lord
> and what his hands have done,
> he will tear them down and not rebuild them.[4]

Similarly, in 22:21 "You have answered me!" is the glad cry that prompts in vv 23–31 the psalmist's anticipation of singing a thanksgiving song.[5]

3. *The thanksgiving song.* A sanctuary setting for the song of thanksgiving is evident from material in the Psalter itself, which in turn supports the view that normally the lament, its precursor, was uttered there. Originally Ps 107 was a psalm for use at a formal service of thanksgiving held during the great pilgrimage festivals, at which the grateful were urged:

> Let them offer thanksgiving sacrifices
> and recount in loud song what he has done . . . .
> Let them extol him in the congregation of the people . . . .
>   (vv 22, 32)

Ps 100 was employed for this same purpose according to its heading, "a psalm for the thank offering." Evidently it functioned as a processional hymn inaugurating the service. The formula that appears in both 100:4, 5 and 107:1, "Give Yahweh thanks, for his goodness, for the everlastingness of his loyal love," supports such a setting. In Jer 33:11 it is described as the joyful cry of worshipers participating in the thank offering service.

Ps 103 with its celebration of God's steadfast love seems to have been a solo hymn sung on such an occasion. Ps 116 makes explicit mention of the service as an opportunity of testifying before the assembled congregation to what God had done, praising him directly in song, and offering a libation and sacrifice of thank offering in the temple courts, while 30:11 highlights dancing. Part of the celebration was a fellowship meal using the meat of the thank offering, which the worshiper enjoyed with his family and friends according to Deut 12:17, 18 and Ps 22:26.

4. *The hymn and other temple poems.* It is not difficult to envisage the hymns as generally functioning in a choral and congregational setting. A number of hymns refer to the music and song that resounded in temple worship, such as 33:1–3:

> Exult in the Lord, you who are righteous . . . !
> Praise the Lord with a lyre.
> Make music for him with a ten-stringed harp.
> Sing to him a new song;
> play beautifully with a joyful sound.

There are informal versions of the songs of Zion, Pss 84 and 122, which attest the joy of pilgrimage to the temple. Pss 24 and 132 preserve references to a sacred procession to the temple, in which the ark was carried. The entrance liturgy of

Ps 15 lets us hear a priest's answer to a would-be worshiper at the temple who inquires about moral qualifications for worship. The ancient custom surely inspired the similar challenge in the Sermon on the Mount, at Matt 5:23, 24, to settle squabbles before worshiping God. In Pss 91 and 121 we overhear the priest dismissing the pilgrim with a powerful word of benediction.

It is clear that the Psalms must be read with controlled imagination in order to compensate for the general lack of precise rubrics. Reconstruction of the institutional setting of many of the psalms, with the help of evidence scattered inside and outside the Psalter, brings them to life. Sympathetic study transforms the flatness of the printed page into three-dimensional fullness, and its silence into voices echoing in the temple courts. The settings help to shed light on the theological meaning of the Psalter which is to be discussed in later chapters. For now, we may reflect on the strong institutional flavor that pervades many of the Psalms.

The institution of the temple obviously lies at the heart of the faith evident in the Psalter. Here was a people that did "not neglect to meet together" (Heb 10:25) but found encouragement in frequenting the sanctuary that symbolized the religious unity of Israel.

"How good, to be sure, how fine it is for brothers to stay together!" exclaimed the psalmist in wonderment at the concourse of pilgrims who had come for the festival (133:1). For them it was a place of joy and fellowship. The institution was not remote from human realities. It satisfied their needs and amply met their expectations. It provided secure refuge and strong assurance when they voiced their cries of distress there; as well, it afforded an opportunity for testimony and praise when the tide of life turned in their favor. The temple was a place where human experience found corresponding religious expression, instead of having a deaf ear turned to fundamental personal and social concerns. Israel in its humanity met with God via the forms and ceremonies of the temple courts, and went away transformed and blessed. Here surely are criteria for the institutional structures of the Christian faith, of whatever denominational flavor, to check whether they are of God. If so, the Christian "house of God" will be a meeting place with him and an indispensable fountain of deep faith:

How precious is your lovingkindness, O God,
that human beings find refuge in the shadow of your wings.
They are refreshed from the rich provision of your house,
and you make them drink from the river of your delights.
For with you is the fountain of life;
and in your light we shall see light! (36:7-9)

Wisdom settings

Certain psalms were not composed with the temple in view. The wisdom psalms have their roots in quite a different setting, which is shared by the better known wisdom literature, Proverbs, Job, and Ecclesiastes. The setting is the world of the wisdom teacher. Religious authority in Israel lay in three quite diverse areas according to Jer 18:18, the spheres of the priest, the prophet, and the wisdom teacher. From these areas stemmed the eventual Old Testament canon of law, prophets, and writings. Wisdom teaching had a theology and ethical system of its own, though these overlapped with the covenant traditions of Israel. It investigated the questions posed by human experience and endeavored to relate the individual to society, and both to God. It possessed distinctive forms of expression, which makes it practicable to recognize wisdom terminology and themes in the Psalter.

1. *Wisdom psalms proper.* There are only a handful of what one might call pure wisdom psalms: Pss 37, 49, 112, and 127. Their habitat was presumably the social setting of

wisdom literature. Unfortunately little is known about this setting, although teaching and discussion were clearly cornerstones of its existence. It was the ancestor of Judaism's rabbinic movement and of the Talmudic school attached to every medieval synagogue.

2. *Wisdom psalms for the temple.* More in number are psalms composed for temple use which betray wisdom influence to a greater or lesser extent: examples are Pss 32, 34, 73, and 111.

3. *Torah-wisdom psalms.* A third category is most interesting. It comprises Pss 1, 19—at least, vv 7–14—and 119, and so has the distinction of providing the first psalm and the longest psalm. These so-called Torah-wisdom psalms reflect a late development of wisdom thinking that wedded the separate concerns of wisdom and of the Torah. Torah is often rendered "law" but it has a wider connotation of divine revelation. Literally meaning "pointing the way," it has the sense of giving directions for the road of life. An important feature of the Torah-wisdom psalms is their stress upon meditation:

Blessed is the man who has not walked in the counsel
of the wicked . . .
But in the Lord's Torah is his delight
and in his Torah will he muse by day and night. (1:1, 2)

The placing of Ps 1 at the head of the whole collection of the Psalter, with the obvious function of an introduction, is highly significant. It represents a loosing of the temple psalms from their institutional moorings and gives them a new role as sacred poems for private devotion and group discussion

For Judaism this new tradition was one of the positive factors that permitted it to survive after the temple was destroyed in A.D. 70. As for Christian usage, this final stamp on the Psalter anticipates and justifies centuries of devotional usage in the realms of homiletics and literature as well as in the private place of prayer and spiritual reflection. In its final form the Psalter becomes a collection of sacred literature released to individuals worldwide as a divine light for the path of life. James Gilmour, a Victorian missionary to Mongolia, spoke for many when he wrote:

> When I feel I cannot make headway in devotion, I open the Psalms and push out my canoe and let myself be carried on the stream of devotion that flows through the whole book. The current always sets toward God and in most places is strong and deep.

The changing scenes of life

Walter Brueggemann has provided a key to the Psalms in his development of an insight perceived by the hermeneutical scholar Paul Ricoeur, and his application of it to the Psalter.[6] What follows borrows from and builds upon his work. It has managed to put on an academic and existential basis what saints down the ages have known instinctively and devotionally, that the Psalms are treasures dug deep from the mines of human life. The value of the Psalter is that it mirrors a broad spectrum of human experience. Life may be divided into three phases, orientation to the world around, disorientation, and reorientation. The Psalms too bear witness to these phases. Expressing the characteristically different moods and feelings of the phases, they relate them to a God who is above them all but sympathetically alert to the instability of the human frame:

> For he knows our make-up,
> he is mindful that we are dust.
> Man is as shortlived as grass.
> He blossoms as briefly as a wild flower . . . .
> But Yahweh's loyal love stays from age
> to age upon those who revere him . . . . (103:14–17)

When the sun is shining and the ship of life is running on a smooth course, there are psalms to read that turn the happy cry "God's in his heaven—all's right with the world" into a song of praise to God as the giver of all good things. Such psalms will be of little use, even mockingly hurtful, when the skies darken and life's frail bark founders in the storm, nor are they meant to be relevant then. That is when despair, which finds its outlet—and begins to find its resolution—in the aggrieved cry "'Do you not care if we perish?'" (Mark 4:38), has a counterpart in the psalms of disorientation. When the storm is over and life returns to an even keel, yet another group of psalms comes into its own, nudging relief and renewed optimism into thanksgiving and praise to God; these are the psalms of reorientation.

These three categories of psalms are closely allied with the very types taught by form criticism and show how unerringly those various types relate to the gamut of human experience, clothed though they are in the dress of a particular culture. The different stylistic forms dovetail with human fortunes. The diligent student can turn what might have seemed the stones of sterile scholarship into the bread of life, as each day requires.

1. *The psalms of orientation.* These may be detected by a telltale motto that runs through a surprising number of form-critical categories and brands them as of the same stock. The hymn to God as Creator declares in tones of awesome praise:

> You are the one who founded the earth . . .
> so that it cannot move for ever and ever. (104:5)

The various hymn subgroups take up the cry. The hymn of divine kingship affirms:

> Yea, the world is established; it shall never be moved;
> thy throne is established from of old. (93:1, 2)

The song of Zion applies the message of Jerusalem:

> God is in its midst—it will not slip!
> God will help it at the break of dawn. (46:5)

The hymn-like variety of royal psalm makes the confident assertion:

For the king is trusting in the Lord
and in the lovingkindness of the Most High, he will not be
   shaken. (21:7)

The entrance liturgy promises to the person who honors the moral requirements of the sanctuary:

> The one doing these things shall not be shaken forever.
>   (15:5)

The psalm of priestly benediction gives a pledge of God's care to the pilgrim leaving for home:

> He will not let your foot stumble. (121:3)

A psalm of normative wisdom pronounces about the righteous person:

> Never will he be shaken. (112:6)

Finally, an affirmation of trust declares of God:

> Because he is my right hand, I shall not be shaken. (16:8)

The motto earmarks these various technical categories, identifying them as psalms of orientation, except that in the case of the affirmations of trust only Ps 16 is clearly included in this group.

The psalms of orientation all move within the theological orbit of divine blessing. It is noticeable that in most cases the motto of stability is carefully safeguarded from any suspicion of humanistic self-sufficiency. The truth is not that a person is fine, but that he or she owes the fine condition to God. For the psalmists nothing in this world has an innate stability but only a derived, God-given one. The national institutions of the temple and the monarchy and even the universe are solid and have lasted for centuries—and look like lasting for centuries longer—simply because they are judged to be expressions of the divine will and so share something of divine stability. For the orientation psalm, life is permeated by God's good will, a factor that is never ignored. According to this perspective a happy life guards itself from the temptation of forgetting God and claiming to be self-made—of which Deut 8:11–18 gives pastoral warning. Rather, it relates constantly to the Giver. Ps 16:8 prefaces the motto of stability with an accompanying attitude of faith: "I have always put the Lord in front of me."

It would be easy to despise the psalms of orientation. It is true that there is danger in going along with the status quo and enjoying it for its own sake. With hindsight the phase of orientation can be seen to include elements of smugness and self-delusion. Each of the phases has its pitfalls.

There is an opposite danger, however, of writing off broad tracts of human experience. The many psalms that reflect this phase are true to life in that they correspond to the periods of comparative stability that occur in the lifetimes of most people. Moreover, the psalms of orientation have standards to live up to and ideals to aim at. The motto "I shall not be moved" does not imply "I shall not move"! The Hebrew terminology connotes stability, not stagnation. Indeed, 16:11 prayerfully affirms that in such seasons "you make me to know the path of life". There is to be movement in a God-ordered direction. An advantage of the period of orientation is that the human heart, at leisure from itself, can look away, wonder at the phenomena of the world around, and reflect insightfully on them, along the lines of 104:34:

> May my reflections please him,
> as I have rejoiced in Yahweh.

The shock of disorientation certainly has a creative effect eventually, but orientation finds creativity in its own steady progress.

2. *The psalms of disorientation.* Clouds of imperfection scud across every blue sky of human orientation. There come times in most lives, however, when the noonday sun turns to darkness and the heavens fall in cataclysm. The communal and individual laments are reactions to such dire crisis, when one's bearings are lost and one cannot cope. It is for this reason that extremes of language and logic occur in them. They are in no way intended as models for prayer offered during a period of orientation. The two calamities that find clear expression in the individual laments are *persecution* and *serious illness*. The latter blow continues to bedevil human society despite leaps in medical knowledge. Persecution, as a type of social alienation, has counterparts in personal crises prevalent in modern times, such as loss of employment, bereavement, and marriage breakdown.

At such junctures the individual laments are the voices of men and women who have been there before us and have wrestled with the agonizing eclipse of the stability that was synonymous with life. There came a time when the bastions of human life, hitherto hailed as mountains of immovability, crumbled and fell. The communal laments of Pss 74 and 79 react to the fall of Jerusalem, temple and all. The royal lament of Ps 89 is aghast at the impending fall of the Davidic monarchy, in the light of divine promises of permanence.

In the laments there is no triumphalism that can readily

exorcize the evil. Nor is there a stoic passivity that grits its teeth and rests patiently in the inscrutable will of God. Instead, one finds the gamut of human emotions that make up the sequence of human reactions to crisis: numb shock, denial of the painful reality, depression and frustration-ridden anger, in fact, all the stages which have to be lived with and through until the final stage, a moving forward in expectation of a new phase of life. In a situation of human misery the psalms of disorientation are companions that understand—unlike Job's misnamed comforters—and behind them stands the God of compassion who knows our frame and somehow is there in the darkness. The admirable quality of Israel's religion is that it had institutional room for the human realism exposed by trauma, witnesses though the laments were to the inadequacy of religious and other institutions and the breakdown of faith as conventionally understood.

3. *The psalms of reorientation.* Life goes on, and in very many cases turns the corner. The song of thanksgiving envisages the dynamic intervention of God in the human situation. Recovery from serious sickness and rehabilitation into society were readily interpreted as answers to prayer, in the light of the oracle that followed the lament. Accordingly the change for the better called for an expression of gratitude to a God who picks up the broken pieces and puts them back together again. One song of thanksgiving, Ps 30, looks back over the three experiences of life, the old orientation in vv 6-7a, the trauma of disorientation expressed via a lament in vv 7b-10 and the now all-encompassing experience of reorientation in vv 1-5 and 11-12:

I said in my security:
"I will never be moved!"
. . . you made me stand more erect than the mountain. . . .
You hid your face—I was dismayed! . . .
You have changed my wailing to dancing for me. . . .

There is a radical note about both the lament and the song of thanksgiving that binds them together: they attest an emotional nadir and zenith in human experience. The thanksgiving song gives voice to an emotional high, just as the lament expresses an emotional low. A temporary factor marks the song of thanksgiving, related as it is to a specific service of thank offering. Yet the song of thanksgiving also marks the beginning of a new experience. There is a debt to God which no single song can discharge. Praise, to be adequate, must be lifelong, characteristically declared the thanksgiving song:

O Lord my God, I will praise you for ever. (30:12)

There is a new sense of commitment to God as dynamic deliverer, which is expected to leave its mark on future living.

Justice must be done to the temporary and permanent qualities of the song of thanksgiving. Perhaps it may be compared to the love letter written during an ardent courtship that eventually is to mature into satisfying marriage and parenthood. The ardor of romantic emotions will not survive the first year or so of marriage, but the underlying truths it expresses remain perennially valid. Accordingly the song of thanksgiving representing reorientation gives voice to the excited beginnings of new life rising from the ruins of personal crisis. The phase is destined to give way to a more settled one which will be both like and unlike the phase of old orientation. Like, in that it will be marked by the stability, steady progress, and appreciation of life enjoyed before. Unlike, in that it will reflect a maturer faith that has found in tragedy and survival schooling in wisdom, and wrested out of them a deeper relationship with God.

The psalm of orientation stands outside the phases of

disorientation and reorientation, which belong back to back as expressions of the need and gift of deliverance. The Songs of Zion, a grouping with similar theme and theology, were sung seemingly before and after the Exile: it was not regarded as foolish that they should be used after the restoration of a ruined city and sanctuary. Accordingly the orientation psalms can give expression to precrisis and postcrisis experiences. The Psalms express the latter truth in theological language: the blessing associated with orientation follows the salvation celebrated in reorientation. After redemption from Exile came resettlement in the land (107:1-3, 33-42). "Deliver your people and bless your inheritance" (28:9) was a fitting sequence of petitions.

> Victory belongs to the Lord.
> Your blessing is upon your people. (3:8)

Orientation can be experienced as a low-lying valley or a high plateau. The steady road up and toward heaven invests everyday life with a spiritual interpretation, whether its stability be of an older or newer variety.

There is a realism about the Psalms that should commend them to a generation which with some justification accuses the church of turning a blind eye to the actualities of human life and failing to integrate experience and faith. The Psalter comes face to face with human experience and does not shrink from verbalizing it and relating it to a kaleidoscope of divine truth. The measure in which Christians find the blatancy of the laments embarrassing is the measure by which they must judge their own openness to life. The Psalms function as honest gauges of human experience. Whatever a person's lot, he or she can read a group of psalms with which to find rapport and a route to God. John Calvin in the preface to his commentary on the Psalms well described the Psalter as an anatomy of all the parts of the soul, for there is not an emotion of which anyone can be conscious that is not here represented as in a mirror. Or rather, the Holy Spirit has here drawn to the life all the griefs, sorrows, fears, doubts, hopes, cares, perplexities, in short, all the distracting emotions with which the minds of men are wont to be agitated.[7]

3   PRAISE

The book of Psalms owes its English title to the Greek version of the Old Testament via the Latin Vulgate. It was obviously derived from an element in the headings of many Psalms, the very term *psalm*, which in Hebrew refers to a composition sung to the accompaniment of a stringed instrument. The title was already current in the New Testament, for instance in Luke 24:44. It evokes the music of the temple and the use of the Psalms in temple worship.

In the Hebrew Bible the title is quite different, and at first sight is a misnomer. It is *sepher tehillim* "book of praises" or simply *tehillim* "praises." The latter term is related to the liturgical exhortation "Hallelujah," "praise Yah(weh)." It occurs in the singular, *tehilla*, as a heading to Ps 145, and could be regarded as the equivalent of the form-critical category of the hymn, although in 22:25 it refers to a song of thanksgiving. Similarly Philo of Alexandria referred to the book of Psalms in Greek as *humnoi* "hymns."

From a form-critical perspective it appears most unreasonable to fasten on one category out of many in choosing an overall title for the Psalter. An editorial note refers to the Davidic collections in Pss 1–72 as "prayers," which may likewise stand for "laments" although these are a form of prayer restricted to the phase of disorientation. Numerically there are a few less hymns, of various types, than laments in the book of Psalms. Laments amount to as much as a third of the Psalter and so might have a better claim as a title if major representation were the criterion. Why, then, was the Hebrew book labeled "praises"?

An important factor is that laments predominate only in the first half of the total collection, in Books One and Two. In the second half there is a preponderance of hymns. This leaning toward praise as the book becomes more complete seems to be due not simply to a desire to redress the balance but to a conviction that "man's chief end is to glorify God," as the Shorter Catechism enjoins.

An editorial concern

1. *The doxologies.* The presence of the doxologies, which in the final edition conclude Books One to Five of the Psalter, is evidence of a yearning to praise God. It is characteristic of the Israelite hymn that praise is not rendered to God for its own sake, as in some modern choruses. Rather, it is grounded in explicit reasoning, for instance in Ps 117:

> Praise Yahweh . . . ,
> because his loyal love has towered over us
> and Yahweh's faithfulness is everlasting.

At first sight the doxologies break the pattern by not giving grounds for praise. In fact, each Book preceding the doxology is regarded as a multitude of good reasons for praising God. The doxology responds to those reasons with its call to praise and its congregational "Amen." Likewise, the bombardment of calls to praise in the final Ps 150 is a reaction to the mass of praiseworthy material to be found in the preceding psalms.

2. *Praise in Book Five*. Gerald H. Wilson has convincingly demonstrated the praise-oriented structure of Book Five of the Psalter.[8] Its forty-four psalms seem to fall into three sections: Pss 107-117, 118-135, and 136-150. Each section has a core of psalms, the first and third being two groups of Davidic psalms, Pss 108-110 and 138-145, and the second the Songs of Ascents, Pss 120-134. Each of the three sections uses an initial formula of praise and a separate final one. Pss 107, 118, and 136 begin their sections with the formula "Give Yahweh thanks for his goodness, for the everlastingness of his loyal love." As we have seen, this formula properly and originally belonged to the thank offering service. In time it also became a general ascription of praise and was taken over into the hymn. By way of climax the initial formula of Ps 136 is reinforced by the refrain that repeats its last part: "for his loyal love is everlasting."

Correspondingly, each of the three sections in Book Five ends with Hallelujah psalms, namely Pss 111-117, 135, and 146-150. These psalms are ones which commence and/or conclude with the added liturgical call "Hallelujah." The alert reader will note that Ps 114 has no Hallelujah. Why not? The reason lies in a tradition, for which there is abundant textual evidence, that it should be combined with Ps 115. These editorial techniques, used to indicate the extent of sections within a larger collection, attest the key role of praise. Praise is the fitting note on which to begin and to end, the A and Z of good psalmody.

3. *Remodeled psalms*. Ps 106 illustrates further an editorial emphasis on praise. Despite keenly argued attempts to classify it as a hymn, it is better identified as a communal lament, especially in view of the petition and vow of praise in v 47, which mark its climax.[9] Hymnic elements there

certainly are in the psalm, but they have been used in the
service of the lament, as often happens. The psalm's perspective has been altered from lament to praise by two
factors: the framework of Hallelujahs, with which the
psalm has been supplied in vv 1 and 48, and the added
doxology, which the framework interpreted as a hermeneutical key to the psalm. Accordingly, the elements of praise
are highlighted over against those of prayer. These elements are certainly worth pushing to the fore; already they
have an important function in the basic psalm. There is a
double stress on God's steadfast love, at beginning and end
(vv 1, 7, 45), and a triple mention of his role as savior in vv
4–10, 21, and 47.

A similar phenomenon has occurred in Ps 115. Again, it is
basically a communal lament or more strictly a liturgy of
lament. The Hallelujah postscript and its incorporation into
its present grouping of Hallelujah Psalms indicate a change
in the balance of emphasis toward the existing elements of
praise. The anti-idolatry satire in vv 4–8 is an implicit confession of praise to the true God, which serves to amplify the
positive praise in v 3. The concluding ascription of praise in
vv 16–18 celebrates his transcendent power as the sole God
who has a unique and exclusive claim to human expressions
of praise:

> Heaven is Yahweh's heaven,
> but the earth he has entrusted to mankind.
> The dead cannot praise Yah(weh) . . . .
> But we will bless Yah(weh)
> from now on and for evermore.

The overall effect of these editorial emphases on praise is
that of a red-letter Bible in which certain material is forced
upon the reader's attention by making it stand out from

seemingly less important content. The result is a playing down of the human situation, so crucial at an earlier level of the Psalter, and a focus upon the person and work of God.

Ps 107 is another instance of reinterpretation with similar intent, although it is carried out in a different manner.[10] As noted earlier, it was originally sung at the thank offering service. Like Ps 100, which was a "psalm for the thank offering," as its heading says, it functioned as a general and communal introduction before individuals took their distinctive part in the service. Ps 107 begins with the thanksgiving formula attested in Jer 33:11:

> Give Yahweh thanks for his goodness,
> for the everlastingness of his loyal love.

It continues with a dramatic description of four kinds of possible danger that might lie behind the discharge of vows at the service: losing one's way in the wilds, imprisonment, dire illness, and shipwreck. So it is tied to personal and specific experiences, to which glad testimony might be made in a public setting. Like the song of thanksgiving, this related composition is open toward general praise. However, Ps 107 in its present form has been transformed into a hymn proper. Verses 2, 3 have been inserted:

> Let Yahweh's redeemed ones say so,
> whom he has redeemed from the enemy's power,
> gathering them from other countries,
> from east and west,
> from north and overseas.

This insertion and also the addition of vv 33–43 turned the psalm into a celebration of the return from Exile— comparable with the "redemption" of the Exodus—and of the resettlement in the land of promise. The rather sensational instances of escape from danger became four descriptions of the release from exile, in two cases focusing upon the national sin that underlay the divine punishment of Exile (vv 11, 17). The purpose of the composition was broadened into communal praise for national salvation and for God's providence that gave a new lease on life in the land.

These cases of reinterpretation are a testimony to the vitality of the Psalms. So treasured were they that they lived on, keeping pace with new situations of God's people and expressing the spirituality of fresh generations of believers who wanted to praise God.

The praise of thanksgiving

1. *Introductory hymns.* Hymnic praise had a key role in the thank offering service. This may be gauged from the processional hymn of Ps 100 and from what was evidently a solo hymn belonging to the same setting, Ps 103. Ps 100 widens the perspective of the service from the individual's enjoyment of God's goodness and steadfast love to a communal experience, membership in the covenant community. Similarly, although Ps 103 begins with characteristic demonstrations of steadfast love that were to be attested in the course of the service—deliverance from sickness and oppression (vv 3–6)—it moves on to the Mosaic revelation of the nature of God. Credal terms are used, which echo Exod 34:6:

> Yahweh is affectionate and dutiful,
> patient and lavish in loyal love. (v 8)

Verses 9–18 are a sermon on this "text." They teach that the loyal or steadfast love which was celebrated as God's chief virtue in the individual testimonies of thanksgiving was perennially at work among his people. The rhetorical calls to praise in vv 19–22 imply that only cosmic adoration might do justice to God's praiseworthiness, but they conclude with the obligation of each individual to join the universal chorale:

> Bless Yahweh, you angels of his. . .
> Bless Yahweh, all his creatures,
> in all places where he rules.
> Bless Yahweh, I tell myself.

The psalmist's self-exhortation is an implicit message to every worshiper at the thank offering service to lift his or her own heart in earnest praise. Let them progress from observation of the joy of others to participation in that contagious joy!

2. *Congregational praise.* The song of thanksgiving was itself by no means devoid of hymnic praise. Just as the term "give thanks" was borrowed by the hymn, so the general term "praise" was employed in the thanksgiving song. This sharing of terms illustrates the degree of overlap in the two types. The public appear to have been encouraged to attend the service of thank offering, just as in many Christian denominations the relatively private sacrament of baptism is regularly celebrated in the presence of the community of faith. The custom served in part to overcome a happy problem experienced by the one who primarily gave thanks. How could he or she express adequately gratitude to God for bounty which meant the difference between life and death? The question is actually posed in 116:12:

> How can I repay Yahweh
> for all his benefits to me?

One solution has been observed in the previous chapter: to praise God throughout the rest of one's life so that life itself would be turned, as it were, into a perennial thank-offering service. In practice this presumably meant regular attendance during festival time at other people's services of thanksgiving and making them one's own. Another solution was to invite the congregation to boost the volume of praise by voicing it on one's own behalf, as in 22:23, 24:

> You who fear the Lord, praise him! . . .
> For he has not despised and has not detested
> the affliction of the afflicted;
> and he has not hidden his face from him,
> but when he cried for help, he heard him.

Parallel cases appear in 32:11 and 118:2–4. The service involved the congregation not simply as silent and perhaps envious spectators of another's good fortune, but as participants whose own hearts were turned to God and whose own lips sang his praises in fresh appreciation.

3. *Singing theology.* This congregational involvement was also served by what is often called the didactic element in the song of thanksgiving; in the first chapter it was referred to as generalized teaching. Such labels are helpful as long as it is realized that in the Psalter learning has praise as its intended end product as well as an appropriate mindset and lifestyle. Statements of a propositional type are regularly represented in the song of thanksgiving. Ps 116 may be used to demonstrate their role. Verse 5 makes a general statement concerning some of God's attributes:

> Yahweh is dutiful and true,
> *our* God shows affection.

In justification of this sweeping statement the psalmist points in v 6a to an activity characteristic of God: "Yahweh takes care of simple folk." Then in v 6b he exposes the personal foundation of this exercise in religious logic: "When I was down, he saved me." The passage seems to establish theology from personal experience, reasoning from what God has just done, to what God habitually does, to what God is. A better way of describing the process would be to say that Israel's theology has found yet another confir-mation in a believer's experience, which provides a testimonial to the character of God. Personal experience is of a piece with traditional theology. The credal statement of v 5, which has its roots in the traditional formulation of Exod 34:6, was here no "commandment of men learned by rote," as Isaiah sadly complained about worship in his day (Isa 29:13 RSV). It had been verified in personal experience. There is a shift from a focus upon that experience to a "pure" theological affirmation. The two are organically linked: thanksgiving is employed as the handmaid of theology.

In another song of thanksgiving, Ps 30, there is a passage which reads like a hymn:

> Sing praise to the Lord, O you saints of his,
> and praise his holy name.
> For in his anger is death,
> but in his favor is life;
> Weeping may tarry in the evening
> but joy comes at dawn. (vv 4, 5)

The final contrast may evoke a night of vigil in the sanctuary until a divine oracle is delivered in the morning. Or it may be a poetic metaphor for the darkness of distress giving way to the glorious light of deliverance. The preceding contrast pits two of God's attributes against each other, anger and favor, in acknowledgment of his sovereign mystery. However, it finds his favor to be the predominant factor and so the focus of communal praise.

Ps 18 is a poem in which thanksgiving and praise oscillate.

It moves backwards and forwards between celebrating the particular experience of salvation and making general statements in praise of God's faithfulness, in vv 20–24, 28, 29 and 32ff on the one hand, and vv 25–27 and 30, 31 on the other. The second half of the psalm begins with a rhetorical question of divine incomparability, which form-critically belongs to the hymn:

> For who is a god, apart from the Lord?
> And who is a rock, except *our* God? (v 31)

The first half of the psalm concludes with an exclamation of praise in v 30: "God—his way is perfect!" The structural highlighting of pure praise is significant. The hymnic passage of 138:4–6 is worth looking up: it likewise gives a key role to praise, placing it at the heart of the psalm.

Praise in the lament

1. *Comfort and challenge.* Not even laments are devoid of praise. Those whose sufferings are expressed in such psalms experienced mental torment. How could they reconcile the God they had known as a friend with a God who was now distant and seemingly alien? The torment comes to a head in the agonized question, why? This question is characteristic of the lament, notably in 22:1, "why have you forsaken me?" However, their previous experience of a positive relationship with God brings a measure of comfort. It brands their present experience as atypical and so, hopefully, temporary. Normal relations would be resumed, it is hoped, because of who God is and because of his ties with the believer as "my God" (22:1).

Reminiscence of God's positive revelation of himself also functions as a challenge to God. Let him intervene and prove himself real and powerful in the present situation, in a manner consistent with previous experience! Psychologically the function of provocative challenge precedes that of comfort, as the negative context of the questions in 77:7–9 suggest:

> Will the Lord spurn for ever,
> and never again be favorable?
> Has his steadfast love for ever ceased? . . .
> Has God forgotten to be gracious? (RSV)

In this latter case the overall context is significant. The challenge follows an expression of nostalgia, seemingly for the historical past celebrated in standard hymns when God revealed himself as savior of the covenant people. Challenge turns to comfort in the second and positive half of the psalm. The Exodus period becomes a theological window through which to glimpse the perennial activity and being of God:

> What god is great like our God?
> Thou art the God who workest wonders. . . .
> (vv 13, 14 RSV)

2. *Remembering God's salvation.* A basic element of the communal lament, occurring early in the composition, is the reference to God's saving activity in the past. An instance is the appeal to God in 74:2:

Remember thy congregation, which thou hast gotten of old, which thou has redeemed to be the tribe of thy heritage!
(RSV)

Ps 44:1–3 is comparable. In the royal lament of Ps 89 the hymn of vv 1–18 and the history of the divine foundation of the Davidic dynasty narrated in vv 19–37 both have a challenging function. The psalmist sets before God his own standards and implicitly urges him to live up to them.

3. *The affirmation of trust.* The communal and individual laments possess a standard element of praise that defines the relationship between God and the individual or community. In Ps 79 the voicing of the relationship constitutes a final appeal: Israel is "thy people, the flock of thy pasture" and so dependent upon their divine patron and shepherd. Praise in the laments is by no means disinterested, nor can it be in its life setting of desperate crisis. It is a weapon in the psalmist's armory, but it owes its sharpness to the truth of God's dynamic being and to the sincerity of the speaker(s)—it is in no way synonymous with flattery. Just as prayer is nothing apart from the reality of a powerful God to pray to, so this form of praise essentially depends upon the objective and subjective reality of the ties between God and believers. In the cry for help which the lament represents, such praise is insisting that God's ability to give help is proven from past experience.

One of the individual laments, Ps 86, makes a propositional statement about God's benevolent, forgiving nature the basis of the appeal for deliverance:

> For thou, O Lord, art good and forgiving,
> abounding in steadfast love to all who call on thee.
>
> (v 5 RSV)

Later the psalmist counters the persecution of his enemies with a fuller form of the same theological proposition:

> But thou, O Lord, art a God merciful and gracious,
> slow to anger and abounding in steadfast love and
> faithfulness. (v 15 RSV)

The "but" of 86:15 is a phenomenon not infrequently found in the individual lament. Claus Westermann has recognized that it introduces a crucial element of praise in the lament.[11]

An affirmation of trust is often so prefaced. It finds in God an ally against misfortune. An example is "But you, O Lord, are a shield around me" (3:3). Craigie well comments:

> If one gazes too long upon the enemy and his might, the enemy grows in the mind's eye to gigantic proportions and his citadels reach up to the skies (Deut 1:28). The hypnotic power of the enemy is broken when one turns one's gaze toward God who is able to fight and grant victory (Deut 1:29, 30).[12]

Other instances worth studying in their context are 13:5; 22:3; 59:8, and 102:12–17. Praise and faith join forces in such affirmations of trust.

4. *Highlighting praise.* In the case of the thanksgiving song it was noticed that in two cases a hymnic passage was put at the heart of the composition (see Pss 18 and 138). The phenomenon is more evident in the lament. There is a tendency to set a hymnic section at the center of a lament:

> O Lord, your lovingkindness is in the heavens,
> your faithfulness reaches to the clouds. . . .
> How precious is your lovingkindness, O God,
> that human beings find refuge in the shadow of your
>   wings. . . .
> For with you is the fountain of life;
> in your light, we shall see light! (36:5–9)

Other cases can be seen in 74:12–17; 80:8–11, and 86:8–13. Pyramid-like, prayer rises to a high point of praise which encapsulates its faith and hope; then it descends, bolstered by the praise. The sequence of prayers, praises, and prayers in Book Two of the Psalter (Pss 42–64, 65–68, and 69–71 [72]), to which Wilson has drawn attention, seems to be a large-scale reproduction of this pattern.[13]

1. *Acrostic theology.* The acrostic or alphabetic pattern used in the case of two hymns, Pss 111 and 145, employs short and relatively independent statements, and so lends itself to theological declarations of a propositional type. Examples are:

> His activity is marked by majesty and splendor,
> and his loyalty continues for ever. (111:3)
> Yahweh is good to all,
> and his compassion covers all his handiwork. (145:9)

This element of praise also occurs in two wisdom psalms which have an acrostic structure, Pss 37 and 112.

2. *Amplifying praise.* The happy problem observed in the case of the song of thanksgiving, the problem of doing justice to God's praiseworthiness, recurs in the hymn. How can God's people praise him enough? One attempted solution is to call for music, for instance in 81:2:

> Raise a song, sound the timbrel,
> the sweet lyre with the harp. (RSV)

Pss 92:3 and 150:3–5 are similar. Another attempt is a rhetorical call to other nations or to the world of humanity, to participate in praise. An example occurs in Ps 117, which celebrates the intimate relationship between God and Israel, yet calls upon "all nations," as if hired choristers, to swell the volume of the praises of Israel, which are not loud enough to do justice to their object:

> Praise Yahweh, all nations . . . ,
> because his loyal love has towered over us. . . .

Ps 100 exhibits a similar phenomenon. Yet praise can never be impersonal or on a "rent-a-crowd" basis. In such cases the rhetorical call seems to imply in plain speech a triumphant claim: "If other nations examine our experience, they will be constrained to acknowledge the reality and power of Yahweh." This understanding is supported by the parallels to the motif in reorientation and disorientation contexts:

> Then it was said among the nations:
> "Yahweh has done a great work
> in his dealings with them." (126:2)
> Why should the nations say,
> "Where is their God?" (79:10; 115:2)

The call to other peoples can be presented in an explicitly provocative way as a rhetorical challenge:

> For great is the Lord, and greatly to be praised;
> he is to be feared above all gods. (96:4 RSV)

The claim is made on the basis of Yahweh's role as Creator (v 5).

Especially impressive is the role of praise imaginatively assigned to the constituent parts of the universe, celestial and terrestrial, inanimate and animate, in Ps 148. Yahweh is envisaged as the praiseworthy focus of all created life and phenomena. All the elements of nature and society owe to him their characteristic essence and function, and to him is due the glory. "Let the gnat make music with the whirring of his wings," as F. B. Meyer paraphrased part of v 10.

At the other end of the scale are the solo hymns. The self-exhortation to praise "Bless Yahweh, my soul," found at the beginning and end of Pss 103 and 104, was meant as a model and incentive for each worshiper—nobody was to be present in body but absent in spirit!

The Psalter is indeed a book of praises. The concentration upon praise that was a dominant concern of editorial activity in the Psalms seems to retreat from their humanness and to concentrate on divineness in a theoretical or at least detached fashion. So be it: this is but one approach among many discernible in the Psalter, and Christianity with its traditional stress on systematic theology cannot cavil. At least, the Psalms are as much concerned with a divine "thou" as with a divine "he." Its theology very often constitutes an awesome confrontation with God. The raw materials of the editorial approach were certainly there to be highlighted.

When St. Paul enjoined the Thessalonian believers to "rejoice always" and to "give thanks in all circumstances" (1 Thess 5:16, 18), was he alluding to the habit of the Psalter to praise in each of life's phases? If so, his exhortation is far from the glib "Hallelujah, anyway" policy advocated by triumphalist preachers. Praise is a constituent part of most of the different types of psalm. With various functions it belongs to all three phases of life, orientation, disorientation, and reorientation. Tate and Brady caught the spirit of the Psalter when they taught the church to sing

> Through all the changing scenes of life,
> In trouble and in joy,
> The praises of my God shall still
> My heart and tongue employ.

The Psalms regularly declare that the dead do not praise God, for instance in 6:5; 30:9, and 115:17. They are affirming that it is the prime function and duty of the living to do so. Human life without praise of God is inconceivable for the Psalter. Praise is the hallmark of true humanity and the fulfillment of human potential.

4 FAITH

Praise and faith are the head and tail of the same penny, the outside and inside of the same pot. They are closely allied as expressions of a godward relation, so that Ps 71 glides easily from mention of "my trust" to that of "my praise" (vv 5, 6). Faith is so pervasive an element in the Psalms that it is difficult to do justice to it: it is the very air that the Psalter breathes. However, a family of words revolves round faith. This range of terms is a fruitful basis of study. Furthermore, the pattern of phases, orientation, disorientation, and reorientation may serve as an organizational model. "Trust in him at all times" (62:8 RSV) is the overall message of the Psalter—in whatever phase of life one happens to be.

Faith in disorientation

It is in the laments that faith flowers most luxuriantly. Disorientation is a period when negativism governs life, outside and within. Doubt, fear, perplexity, and despair are negative reactions spawned by the disintegration of normal life. Ironically faith can feed as well as fight such foes. Why should the believer be beset by crisis?

1. *The protest of faith.* There is a tone of protest and even resentment in 43:2, 3:

> For you are the God of my stronghold;
> why have you rejected me?
> Why must I wander about in darkness . . . ?

A similar sense of perplexity occurs in the communal lament of Ps 44:

> All this happened to us, but we did not forget you
> and we did not act deceitfully in covenant with you.
> Our heart did not turn back
> nor did our foot turn aside from your path. (vv 17, 18)

The passage is provocatively resonant with the language of faith, a true faith that issued in a corresponding lifestyle of obedience. Faith is here loyalty, a sense of commitment to the covenant relationship. Search though they may, the community can see no adequate reason why this crisis should suddenly be sent by God at this time. A cherished set of religious expectations has been shattered, they protest. Life no longer makes sense.

In 22:1 the cry "My God, my God, why have you forsaken me?" makes the same point on the individual level. It continues in a similar vein. Traditional piety taught that trust was the prelude to certain deliverance, and Israel's hymns—"the praises of Israel"—celebrated this truth (vv 3–5), but the psalmist's experience ran counter to this expectation. He could look back on a whole lifetime of commitment to God:

> I was cast upon you from the womb;
> from my mother's belly, you have been my God. (v 10)

Yet it had neither shielded him from the onset of crisis nor brought God rushing to repel the intruder. Not deliverance but disappointment was his lot. Faith received an aching wound.

The experience is an example of the chaos that disorientation stirs up in the human heart. It is devastating because nothing in life is sacrosanct, nothing is able to escape the onslaught unscathed. Disorientation spells the end of life as it was habitually known. Even faith cannot immediately bridge the gap. The very existence of the lament indicates a degree of faith, but underlying it is the all-too-human cry, "I believe, help my unbelief."

2. *The testimony of faith.* Faith is wounded by crisis, but not killed. Yet there is an early stage in disorientation, short or long, when faith in the sense of finding any religious meaning in life is seemingly dead. There is an indication of this experience in some communal laments. The psalm leader breaks into a collective prayer with a solo affirmation of faith in a mighty God. A certain instance is 74:12–17:

> Yet God my King is from of old,
> working salvation in the midst of the earth. . . .
> Thou has fixed all the bounds of the earth;
> thou hast made summer and winter. (RSV)

The reader can look up other passages which appear to have this role, 44:6–8 and 94:16–23. Ps 115:9–11, a priestly exhortation in a liturgy of lament, has a similar function. The impression given is that the leader ventures into paths of assurance where he knows that the congregation cannot yet follow him in honesty. He speaks on his own account as a pastoral comforter of the community, to direct them to a light gleaming in the darkness, which he at least can glimpse. "My God" (44:4; 94:22) or "my King" (44:4; 74:12) has a positive ring: it is an appeal to a continuing relationship.

3. *The appeal of faith.* Ps 31:14 uses the same claim to differentiate between the dire crisis and a factor that spells hope:

> But I—I have trusted in you, O Lord,
> I have said "You are my God."

The psalmist claims protection as a committed "servant" of God, and appeals to "lovingkindness" (v 16) or "steadfast love" (RSV), God's attribute of loyalty to his own. He has believed exclusively in Yahweh and never strayed into pagan religion (v 6). He matches the commitment of the old days of orientation with a new and appropriate commitment: "Into your hand I commit my spirit" (v 5). It fits the phase of disorientation as a desperate turning to God for help.

Ps 86 is worth reading in this connection: the whole of it is similarly resonant with faith that expresses itself within the sphere of a divine-human relationship.

Ps 119, Torah-wisdom psalm though it is, has no ivory tower for its setting, but a situation of stress. In it the poet regularly refers to himself as "your servant" and once to Yahweh as "my God" (v 115). Here typically it is the Torah to which he "cleaves" (v 31) and in which he "trusts" (v 42) and "believes" (v 66).

Ps 7:1 combines the relational address "my God" with a synonym of trust, "I have sought refuge in you." This verbal phrase and the cognate noun "(place of) refuge" are standard psalm language for faith in God. Recourse to God's protective power is the basis of the beautiful prayer in 57:1,

> Be merciful to me . . . ,
> for in thee my soul takes refuge;

in the shadow of thy wings I will take refuge,
till the storms of destruction pass by. (RSV)

The imperative "be merciful" is a relational verb: in Hebrew
thinking it has the connotation of being true to one's obligations to a dependent: 86:2, 3 and 123:2 are worth looking up
and comparing.[14] Ps 59:9, 16 looks forward to the time when
God will be celebrated in thanksgiving as a proven "fortress
and a refuge in the day of my distress." Ps 141:8 describes
this turning to God in faith thus:

> Truly to you, Yahweh, Lord, are my eyes directed.
> In you I seek refuge: do not expose me to death.

In 61:3 an affirmation of trust describes God as "my
refuge, a strong tower against the enemy" (RSV). Prov 18:10
echoes such a formula of commitment when it describes the
name of Yahweh as "a strong tower; the righteous man runs
into it and is safe."

4. *Faith as the answer to fear.* It is this recourse to protective power that proves to be an antidote to natural fear:

> The Lord is the refuge of my life;
> of whom shall I be afraid? . . .
> Even though an army encamps against me,
> my heart shall not fear.
> Even though war rises up against me,
> in spite of this, I am confident. (27:1, 3; cf. 3:3, 6)

Ps 23, an affirmation of trust expanded into a complete
composition, has as its actual or remembered background
the phase of disorientation. It gives a prominent place to the
powerful protection afforded by the presence of God, which
keeps fear at bay. Two word pictures divide the psalm into
halves, the image of the shepherd in vv 1-4 and that of the

Faith

hospitable host in vv 5, 6. On the other hand, two direc-
tional perspectives split the psalm differently, the testimony
or meditation of vv 1–3 with its third-person mention of
Yahweh, and the prayer of vv 4, 5 which employs more
intimate direct address. (The final "Yahweh" in v 6 is a concluding device which returns full circle to its occurrence at
the beginning, v 1.)

The effect of the different groupings is to highlight the
overlapping v 4, with its conviction of the fear-quelling protective presence of God. The throbbing heart of the psalm
lies at this point:

> Even though I shall walk
> through the valley of the shadow of death,
> I fear no evil.
> For thou art with me;
> thy rod and thy staff—
> they comfort me. (RSV)

5. *Faith as certainty.* Trust has a ring of subjective certainty when the verb "know" is used to express it. "This I
know, that God is for me" is the climactic assertion of confidence in 56:9 (RSV). Fear has found natural room in the
psalmist's heart, but his turning to God in trust is able to
dislodge it:

> When I am afraid,
> I put my trust in thee. . . .
> in God I trust without a fear.
> What can flesh do to me? (vv 3, 4 RSV)

To reapply Martin Luther's imagery, he could not stop this
bird landing on his head, but by faith he could prevent it
nesting in his hair. In comparison with his powerful God,
human oppressors are cut down to size as weak "flesh."

There is a looking forward to the announcement of God's positive intervention through a prophetic oracle or "word" (vv 4, 10).

The term "know" is also used as the climax of a lament in a forward-looking context at 140:13:

> I know that Yahweh will undertake
> the cause of the afflicted,
> securing justice for the needy.

The psalmist is here envisaging his own cause as bound up with God's typical vindication of the oppressed. In Israelite theology God is one who rights wrongs and champions the underdog. Herein lies not only the hope of other victimized believers, as v 13 also hints, but also his own hope.

Similar concluding assurance about the future is expressed in an impressive "I believe" at 27:13:

> I believe that I will see the goodness of the Lord
> in the land of the living.

The calm conviction of survival is the corollary of having turned over to God the threats to his life, in the passionate petitions of vv 7–12 which precede. These concluding statements in psalms of lament correspond to the final stage of disorientation. This stage is marked by a positive openness to the future, by a sure hope that there is life out there beyond the cataclysm of crisis. In 13:5, 6 such confidence is expressed with the verb "trust": the psalmist is confident that God will intervene in loyal help ("steadfast love," "salvation") and expects that soon his praying will be changed to praising:

> But I have trusted in thy steadfast love;
> my heart shall rejoice in thy salvation.

Faith

I will sing to the Lord,
because he has dealt bountifully with me. (RSV)

6. *Faith in God's word.* In some laments an extra element
is appended, a reaction to receipt of the desired oracle. It
often includes the language of faith. In 6:8, 9 there is no such
terminology, but the passage glows with confidence that
God's promise of vindication, just given to him, will come
true:

Depart from me, all workers of wickedness,
for the Lord has heard the sound of my weeping.
The Lord has heard my supplication.

In Ps 28 the prophetic oracle seems to be represented in v 5:

Because they do not understand the works of the Lord
and what his hands have done,
he will tear them down and not rebuild them.

Relief at receiving it prompts first an outburst of praise that
the appeal to God to hear prayer (v 2) has been honored, and
then a declaration of faith:

Blessed be the Lord,
for he has heard the voice of my supplications.
The Lord is my strength and my shield;
my heart has trusted in him. (vv 6, 7)

Faith receives a fillip from answered prayer. There is a similar profession at the end of Ps 55. Verse 22b evidently functions as the mediation of a divine response, while v 23
expresses a conviction that God will implement his promise
by punishing his guilty enemies:

He will never permit
the righteous to be moved.
But thou, O God, wilt cast them down
into the lowest pit;
men of blood and treachery
shall not live out half their days.
But I will trust in thee.

The psalmist "trusts" God to vindicate him.

The faith expressed in these answered laments might be called second-degree faith. By contrast the first-degree faith of petitionary lament has been bolstered simply by a prior life of faith and by attendance at the sanctuary where the faith was expressed. The other type of faith has an extra basis, the divine response. Yet it is not to be despised as easy or undemanding. There was still a considerable gap between the divine promise and its eventual implementation in fact. The situation of crisis bewailed in the lament had not yet changed. On returning home the one who had prayed would not find immediate reorientation. By faith, however, he clings to the word given to him, sure that his problems will be resolved. The divine word enables him to return to the old situation with confidence and hope.

Faith in orientation

Faith, in the Psalms, is by no means a foxhole phenomenon, even though its vocabulary is most evident in the laments. Just as the laments make vigorous mention of pre-disorientation faith, so the psalms of orientation speak of faith as the foundation of ordinary life. It does not need crisis to create it.

1. *Faith fosters stability.* The motto of orientation is associated with faith more than once. In Ps 21, a royal psalm, faith is the secret, humanly speaking, of the king's stability:

The king is trusting in the Lord,
and in the lovingkindness of the Most High, he will
not be shaken. (v 7)

This faith is not self-confidence, but a reflection of divine faithfulness, and therein lies its validity. God has established the institution of kingship and is committed to it. There has to be a complementary commitment on the part of the king. It takes the form of faith. Ps 16 attests that the ordinary believer "shall not be shaken" inasmuch as his life is marked by "putting the Lord always before" him (v 8; 54:3 and 86:14 are worth comparing). Here might be mentioned 125:1, although the motto occurs in an affirmation of trust within a communal lament:

Those who trust in Yahweh
are like Mount Zion,
which is immovable, abiding forever.

Faith is again the human means of security. Despite a situation of crisis, in this case life evidently still had a modicum of orientation. This residue of stability encourages expectation of a fuller enjoyment of blessing in the future. The affirmation of 125:1 is applying a motif drawn from the Songs of Zion to the theme of faith. In one of this particular group of hymns God's presence in Zion guarantees its stability:

God is in its midst—it will not slip!
God will help it at the break of dawn. (46:5)

The community's response is one of faith, in a refrain:

The Lord of hosts is with us;
the God of Jacob is our stronghold. (vv 7, 11, cf. v 1)

God's special localization within the temple implies his protective presence with the community. Proof of this is given in a manner typical of the Songs of Zion, a harking back to an archetypal victory won in connection with Jerusalem (vv 5b, 8–10; 48:3–7, and 76:3, 5, 6 are comparable). Luther caught the spirit of the psalm in his hymn "A Mighty Fortress is Our God."

2. *Faith brings blessing*. The informal counterparts of the Songs of Zion, Pss 84 and 122, breathe an atmosphere of faith. Ps 84 culminates in a specific mention of faith: "O Lord of hosts, blessed is the man who trusts in thee!" (v 12 RSV). This appreciative sentiment is a response to the blessings already promised in temple worship and yet to be realized after returning home. Faith in the God of Zion is the door to receiving blessing. It is clear that Israel's religious institutions were incarnational stimuli for faith. They represented God in forms that eyes could see and ears could hear—and feet could walk among:

> Our feet are standing
> within your gates, Jerusalem (122:2).

3. *Faith is commended*. If sacred history provides fuel for faith in Ps 46, it teaches lessons for faith in a hymn that celebrates Yahweh as the Lord of Israel's history, Ps 78. That psalm uses history to warn against having "no faith in God" and not "trust[ing] his saving power" (v 22). It urges each new generation of God's people to learn from history an attitude of faith and obedience:

> so that they should set their hope in God,
> and not forget the works of God,
> but keep his commandments;
> and that they should not be like their fathers . . . ,
> whose spirit was not faithful to God. (vv 7, 8)

Similarly a wisdom poem teaches its hearers to "trust in the Lord and do good" (37:3).

4. *Faith, true and false.* The orientation psalms spell out the direction of faith by differentiating it from substitute forms and warning against them as false. True faith is exclusive and forbids any truck with the idolatry of pagan religion:

> They have acquired another (god).
> I will not pour out their libations of blood,
> and I will not take their names upon my lips.
> (16:4; cf. Job 31:26, 27)

It was observed earlier that an individual lament pleads that such a faith has been a mark of pre-disorientation piety:

> I have hated those who keep vain idols,
> but I have trusted in the Lord. (31:6)

Faith in God also rules out faith in materialism, whether money (see 49:6; 52:7; compare 62:10 and Job 31:24, 25) or armaments (see 20:7 and 33:16; compare 44:6). It also runs counter to an alternative faith in humanity:

> Do not trust in rulers,
> in an earthling who cannot save.
> His breath leaves him, he returns to his native earth:
> on that day his policies have perished.
> How fortunate is the one whose help is Jacob's God,
> whose hope is set on Yahweh as his God. (146:3–5)

5. *Faith ensures deliverance.* In the lament of Ps 22 the traditional religious truth that trust led to deliverance was cited with mingled doubt and hope:

O my God, I cry out by day, but you don't answer . . . .
Our fathers trusted in you;
they trusted and you delivered them. (vv 2, 4)

This truth may be glimpsed in its habitat of orientation in
the benediction of Ps 91. The promise is given to the believer that "because he cleaves to me in love, I will deliver
him" (v 14 RSV). There is a provident admission that the
golden days of orientation may not last forever. Assurance is
given, however, that God's protective power would be at
work in such a case, as Ps 22 is eventually able to acknowledge. Likewise the promise is made in 112:7, 8 that if bad
news comes, the trusting heart will be able to overcome the
paralysis of fear, and if social alienation befalls the believer,
his faith will see him through:

> He is not afraid of bad news:
> his mind is firm, trusting in Yahweh,
> his mind is steady, he will not be afraid
> as he awaits looking at his foes with gratification.

Faith in reorientation

At first sight the psalms of reorientation add little to the
Psalter's theme of faith. But life is like being on an escalator
moving the wrong way: one has to move forward in order to
stay in the same place. So it is a tribute to this particular
phase of life that it promotes a reaffirmation of truths professed in the salad days of orientation and claimed in the dog
days of disorientation. The language may not differ, but the
life of the believer who uses it has been a pilgrimage from
faith to faith.

1. *Faith refueled.* One lament looks forward to the song
of thanksgiving as a celebration of Yahweh's protective
power in personal experience:

> Thou *hast been* to me a fortress
> and a refuge in the day of my distress. (59:16 RSV)

A royal song of thanksgiving begins exuberantly with a piling up of statements of praise which all use the terminology of faith:

> The Lord is my cliff and my stronghold and my deliverer;
> my God is my rock in whom I seek refuge,
> my shield and my horn of salvation, my safe retreat. (18:2)

Here indeed is faith's vindication, which in turn reinvigorates faith.

2. *Faith commended.* Personal experience can have a sequel in the commendation of faith to others, in the teaching style that characterizes the song of thanksgiving: "Blessed is the man who seeks refuge in him" (34:8) and "Blessed is the man who made the Lord his trust" (40:4). In Ps 116 the psalmist declares how right he was to keep his faith during the period of disorientation, when people around him proved so untrustworthy:

> I had faith, even when I declared,
> "I am suffering acutely."
> I said in my alarm,
> "All men are unreliable." (vv 10, 11)

In Ps 118 a grateful king teaches a similar lesson, which experience has just taught him, that recourse to human allies and counselors comes a poor second to trust in Yahweh:

> It is better to take refuge in Yahweh
> than to trust in men.
> It is better to trust in Yahweh
> than to trust in rulers. (vv 8, 9)

3. *Faith lost and won.* Ps 73 is a unique song of thanksgiving in that it celebrates deliverance not from a physical crisis, although that had been no stranger (see v 14), but from spiritual and intellectual doubt. This is what the stumbling of feet means here in v 2, as v 3 explains:

> As for me, my feet had almost stumbled,
> my steps had well nigh slipped.
> For I was envious of the arrogant,
> when I saw the prosperity of the wicked. (RSV)

The song, written from a wisdom perspective, discusses the problem of an unjust providence. The psalmist had discovered the truth shrewdly expressed by John Dryden, that "virtue in distress and vice in triumph make atheists of mankind." In this situation faith and experience were signposts pointing opposite ways. The one thing that stopped him from following the latter road away from God was a sense of commitment not to God himself but to fellow believers:

> If I had said, "I will speak thus,"
> I would have been untrue to the generation of thy
>   children. (v 15 RSV)

Eventually his faith is rekindled, in a visit to the temple, seemingly at festival time when traditional hymns celebrating God's providential judgment were sung. His cold heart is warmed; he is able to apply the hymnic language to the prosperous renegades whom he had envied. He goes on to confess that the materialistic attitude which had had a corrosive effect upon his faith was animal-like, and to exult in a new sense of the reality of God:

> When my soul was embittered, . . .
> I was like a beast toward thee.

Nevertheless I am continually with thee;
thou dost hold my right hand. . . .
but God is the strength of my heart and my portion
for ever. (vv 21–23, 26 RSV)

The logical conclusion of the psalm, expressed in v 1, is: "Truly God is good to [Israel]." At first hearing it sounds trite, but the same language can express a low or high level of faith. Here the spiritual stance is that of Dostoevsky's Christian testimony: "It is not as a child that I believe and confess Christ. My 'hosanna' is born of a furnace of doubt."

5 BLESSING

The motto of the phase of orientation in human life, "we shall not be moved," is a neutrally descriptive statement. In the usage of the Psalter, however, it has a firm theological basis. Not only is faith in God hailed as the secret of a steady life, but the divine origin of such stability is emphasized by grounding it in blessing. The theology of orientation relates to a God who blesses.[15]

Blessing in creation

The reader of the Old Testament is well prepared for the Psalms' association of the theme of blessing with God's role as Creator. He or she has encountered the association at the opening of Genesis, where the narrative of creation makes much of God's pronouncement of blessing, upon animals, humanity, and even the Sabbath day (Gen 1:22, 28; 2:3). A regular theme of the hymns of praise in the Psalter is God's work in creation. Here too it is related to blessing.

Two hymns, Pss 8 and 104, make use of the same traditions as Gen 1 and develop them in tones of praise.

1. *God's viceroys.* Ps 8 celebrates human power over the world, especially over the rest of animate creation. It envisages the pioneer who tames the wilds and brings them under control so that they function as his own environment. Verse 5 affirms:

> Thou hast made him little less than God,
> and dost crown him with glory and honor. (RSV)

Crowning is a general metaphor of blessing in 65:11 and 103:4; in this case the crowning "with glory and honor" paints a more precise picture of king-making. It sets human power in a corrective context of accountability, just as the vassal king crowned by his overlord was not only a sovereign but also a subject. Judah's political history in the late preexilic period included two bitter experiences of the loss of royal independence. Pharaoh enthroned Eliakim, giving him the trappings of nationalistic royalty in the form of a new Yahwistic name, Jehoiakim, and Nebuchadnezzar enthroned Mattaniah as Zedekiah, probably with the same underlying intent (2 Kgs 23:34; 24:17). In Ps 8 an admission that Yahweh is the power behind the human throne is communicated by its frame of praising declarations of God's majesty as king of the world in vv 1 and 9:

> O Lord, our governor,
> how majestic is your name in all the earth.

As in Gen 1:27, 28, it is God who empowers humanity to function as his regent and thus as agent of his will.

2. *God's extended family.* Ps 104 widens the perspective of blessing so that it encompasses not only humanity but the whole of the animate world, just as Gen 1:22, 28 present parallel mandates of blessing to both the animal and human

sectors of creation. The psalm betrays its setting in the sphere of orientation by the version of its motto in v 5: it is because God has founded the earth so firmly that "it cannot move for ever and ever." The world in which humanity finds itself is a safe place to live in, affirms the hymn, because it has a God-given security. By this blessing humanity is set free from a basic anxiety, and in positive terms is free to get on with the work of maintaining and promoting life. It is the human worker who is the concern of the central stanza, vv 14–23. The opening theme of the stanza is human labor in the fields, tending the cattle and producing food and even wine "to gladden the heart." Its closing note is the long day devoted to human labor, from morn to evening. Yet the boon from this toil depends upon initial divine giving: the vegetation for animal and human consumption grows by God's design and at his behest.

In this rural presentation of human life the environment is essentially shared with animals. There is the conception of a divine economy that governs even birds and wild beasts. Mountain terrain beyond humanity's utilitarian concern is prized not for its idyllic beauty but as the habitat of wild goats and conies. Nonproductive trees are regarded as being there for birds to nest in. The division of time into night and day is evidence of God's programmed cycle of activity for animals and humans. Everywhere the psalmist looks he sees signs of an ordered structure which is the gift of a God who blesses. In this representation of the world animals, birds, and humans live together in mutual respect, coexisting and in part cooperating.

The next stanza of the psalm, vv 24–30, celebrates God as maker of all creatures great and small, and as constant supplier of their vital needs. They are portrayed as his family, ever dependent on the benevolent hand of their divine parent for the sustenance of life. He it is who ensures the continuity of life from generation to generation. As one generation dies, he "creates" another with his life-giving energy. There is a dynamic relationship between God and the creatures he has made: apart from his continuous intervention in blessing all life disintegrates and disappears.

3. *God's universal love.* Two other hymns praise God as the regular supplier of food to the world. Language similar to that of Ps 104 is used in 145:15, 16:

> The eyes of all look to you
> and you give them their food in due time.
> You open your hand
> and satisfy the desire of every living being.

In Ps 136:25 the role of God as one "who gives food to all living creatures" backtracks to an earlier theme of the psalm, that of creation, broached in vv 4–9. God's initial work of creation was not a static activity that, once done, left the world to its own devices. It had as its corollary a continuous providence whereby food is given "to all flesh." The refrain of praise that punctuates each declaration made in Ps 136, "for his loyal love is everlasting," has a remarkable use in this context of creation. Normally "loyal love" relates to aspects of God's faithfulness in the covenant relationship with Israel. Here, however, it is widened to his care for all his creatures. The same usage occurs just as strikingly in 145:8, 9, where the formula of Exod 34:6 is extended from a covenant setting to one of universal providence:

> Yahweh is dutiful and compassionate,
> patient and greatly loyal.
> Yahweh is good to all,
> and his compassion covers all his handiwork.

Similarly 33:5 and 119:64 attest that "the earth is full of the Lord's lovingkindness." A covenant attribute has been expanded to cover the faithful relationship that binds the Creator to his creatures in a world that has no independent existence.

This reinterpretation in universal terms has a relevance beyond the Psalter: it recurs as the theological fulcrum of the book of Jonah (Jon 4:2). From a long-term perspective it brings the reader of the Bible a good step closer to the universal love of God celebrated in the New Testament, which integrates the covenantal and universal meanings of "steadfast love" found in the Old. Yet it serves to warn the Christian against a form of otherworldliness that despises the natural world of space and the senses. In these psalms God's steadfast love has become part of the vocabulary of material blessing, for which Israel gives thanks not as the chosen people but as part of the human race.

4. *God's enabling.* Another hymn, Ps 29, makes God's control over the forces of nature the basis for more particular assurances:

> The Lord will give protection to his people;
> the Lord will bless his people with peace. (v 11)

Because of his lordship over nature he is able to care effectively for his own. There is a hymnic formula describing Yahweh as "maker of heaven and earth" which in the Psalms links blessing for Israel or for its individual members with his work in creation. Seemingly it had deep roots in ancient worship at Jerusalem, for it is used in the benediction spoken to Abraham by the Jebusite priest-king Melchizedek (Gen 14:19). Ps 115:15 is part of a priestly benediction issued to the congregation in the temple courts: "May you be blessed by Yahweh, maker of heaven and earth." By right of creation Israel's God controls the world, and by this power he is able to do more than his people can ever ask. This is the power that is reassuringly invoked as the generous measure of his blessing. In 121:2 it is characterized as "help" that undergirds the daily life of the believer:

> The source of my help is Yahweh,
> maker of heaven and earth.

Blessing in worship

A blessing similar to that in Ps 115, given in the name of the "maker of heaven and earth," is uttered in 134:3 as a blessing "from Zion." Similar, but without the creation formula, is the benediction of 128:5, "May Yahweh bless you from Zion." These references indicate how closely blessing is linked with the temple. Indeed, 133:3 makes the categorical statement that Zion "is where Yahweh has ordered the blessing to be." Lev 9:22, 23 and 2 Chr 30:27 suggest that in Israelite tradition an act of sacrificial worship concluded with a priestly benediction. Luke 1:21, 22 alludes to this tradition as part of the priestly duties of Zechariah, the father of John the Baptist. On certain occasions the king exercised this priestly role, according to 2 Sam 6:18. Ps 24 appears to refer to divine blessing as the sequel to worship in the sanctuary (vv 3, 5):

> Who shall ascend into the mountain of the Lord
> and who shall stand up in his holy place? . . .
> He will receive blessing from the Lord. . . .

It is presumably not coincidental that the last of the Songs of Ascents concludes with a benediction (134:3).

1. *The mutuality of blessing.* One can speak of a cycle of blessing, for the term "bless" is also used of the praise that Israel offers in worship. There is an interchange of the two kinds of blessing in Ps 134. There is first a call, evidently to the congregation standing in the temple courts, to "bless" or

praise Yahweh, raising their hands toward the temple as a gesture of worship. Then another cry rings out, invoking divine blessing upon those who bless him. The cycle of blessing to and from God reminds the Christian of Eph 1:3, "Blessed be the God and Father of our Lord Jesus Christ, who has blessed us in Christ with every spiritual blessing. . . ." (RSV). In Ps 134 the order is based on religious practice whereby worship was concluded with a benediction. God's blessing is the gracious byproduct of worship.

2. *The theology of benediction.* In Num 6:24–26 there is a prescribed form of words which has been carried over into Christian worship: "The Lord bless you and keep you; the Lord make his face to shine upon you . . . and give you peace." The interpretive comment on the benediction in v 27 is significant: "So shall they put my name upon the people of Israel, and I will bless them." It suggests that the priestly benediction, uttered in the form of petitionary wishes, would be followed by Yahweh's implementation of the benediction. Divine blessing was not simultaneously mediated through the human words. Rather, Yahweh heard and honored the formal wishes of his ministers by bestowing blessing upon the subsequent lives of his worshipers. Both divine sovereignty and the implicit power of the benediction find expression here. Evidently the priestly benediction, although generally expressed in the form of wishes, by grace has the virtual force of a promise, like a check which is subsequently honored. This procedure sheds light on 115:12–15, where the multiple assurance that Yahweh will bless is followed—strangely at first sight—by a benediction in wish form:

> May you be blessed by Yahweh,
> maker of heaven and earth. (v 15)

The passage makes good sense, for the benediction carries with it a divine undertaking that God would honor it.

3. *A promise kept.* Ps 67:1, "May God be gracious to us and bless us and make his face to shine upon us" (RSV) echoes part of the benediction formula of Num 6:24-26. Seemingly God's dutiful compliance with the covenant relationship and his smile of favor are here invoked in a prayer for blessing rather than in a benediction. If so, the relation of the prayer to the rest of the psalm is by no means clear.

It may be the case, as some scholars consider, that the Hebrew verbs are intended as imperfect and refer to God's habitual attitude: "God is customarily gracious to us and makes his face. . . ." The psalm then expresses gratitude for blessing received, specifically in the harvest (v 6), and gives praise that God is one who honors the benediction uttered in his name. The imperfect form of the Hebrew verbs in the repeated clause of vv 6, 7, with the apparent sense "God blesses us" lends some support to this interpretation.

4. *Pledges to pilgrims.* Another echo of the Aaronic benediction occurs in Ps 121, with its sixfold use of the verb "keep." The setting is best explained as the imparting of a priestly blessing to a pilgrim before he leaves the holy city at the end of a festival. His own conviction of faith, taught to him by his period of worship, is clinched by a priestly or prophetic voice in vv 3-8, speaking in tones of solemn promise. The promise begins with the motto of orientation expressed in a form which places the onus for its implementation upon God: "He will not let your foot stumble; . . ." Ps 91 may have originated in a similar setting. The "shelter of the Most High" and "shadow of the Almighty" (v 1) then refer to recourse to the temple in demonstration of the pilgrim's faith. The kernel of the official promise is vv 9, 10:

> Because you have made the Lord your refuge,
> the Most High your habitation,
> no evil shall befall you,
> no scourge come near your tent.

Worship at the temple is crowned with a promise that in consequence orientation will be the pilgrim's lot, and disorientation will be kept at bay.

Blessing in everyday life

The benediction builds a bridge between worship and returning to pick up the threads of everyday life. The pilgrim set out on his return journey with rich assurances of blessing ringing in his ears. It is easy to see from the phenomenon of the benediction how essential the institution of the temple was for the life of the Israelite. He met with God in temple worship; this God goes back with him into the secular world, preserving, protecting, and prospering:

> Yahweh is your guardian,
> Yahweh is your protection
> at your right hand. (121:5; cf. 16:8; 91:15)

1. *Life sustained and fulfilled.* Blessing essentially spells life and the perpetuation of life; it is defined in 133:3 as "life for evermore." Human existence was much less cushioned than in modern Western society. Harm loomed time and again, and threat of harm even more. "Guard me" or more basically "keep me," is the petition in 16:1, in a psalm which most probably has a setting of orientation. The earnest request takes up a term belonging to the priestly benediction. It reminds God to act in compliance with his promise and trustfully expects that he would do so. To stay alive and fit to work would be bounty indeed. Not to be given up to Sheol in death (v 10) was a prospect worthy of praise. To be directed by God, so as to enjoy life and its pleasures, was veritable blessing:

> You make me to know the path of life,
> the full rejoicing of your presence,

the perpetual pleasantness by your right hand.
(v 11; see Eccl 3:12, 13; 9:9)

Another term belonging to the vocabulary of blessing is usually rendered "peace," but is perhaps more accurately defined as fulfillment. This term occurs at the end of the benediction in Numbers 6:24–26. It appears in blessing contexts in the Psalter, such as at 29:11, "The Lord will bless his people with peace" (cf. 128:6; 147:14).

There is a useful definition of the range of blessing in Ps 144. In vv 12–14 the people offer prayerful wishes for what the RSV loosely paraphrases in v 15 as "blessings." They comprise sturdy sons and daughters, good crops, flocks that lamb well, and healthy, well-fed cattle. These were the natural concerns of the post-exilic community as it endeavored to build up a stable and strong society in the face of great odds. There was a prayerful expectation that God would meet them at the very point of these needs.

In contexts of blessing, the concern for children, as befits a seriously underpopulated society, appears often, for instance in 107:38; 115:14; 147:13, while the expression of dependence on God for crops is reflected in 67:6; 132:15 and 147:14. In the difficult economic conditions of the post-exilic period especially Judah needed all the help and morale building it could get. The help that Yahweh could give was taken seriously.

2. *Dependence on God.* This factor of support from Yahweh is well expressed in a description of Yahweh that applies to all of life's phases, whether orientation (16:5), disorientation (119:57; 142:5; cf. Lam 3:24) or reorientation (73:26).

He is "my portion," attests the believer concerning the God who blesses. The origin of the phrase is generally seen in the phenomenon that the tribe of Levi had no portion of land allotted to them but instead depended for their sustenance on gifts and offerings made to Yahweh. In the Psalter the term has been spiritualized, but not so as to exclude the material sphere. It is Yahweh who is the believer's sustenance, his ultimate life-support system and the source of all that fulfills his potential. Ps 1:3 insists that steady growth in life depends intrinsically upon God, encountered through the Torah:

> So shall he be like a tree, . . .
> which shall yield its fruit in its season,
> and its foliage shall not wither.
> So, in all that he shall do, he shall prosper.

A religion which has such concepts of blessing cannot be accused of being preoccupied with the soul. In this religion God has a key role in all the enterprises of human life, in its goings out and comings in (see 16:7, 8 and 121:8; see also Deut 28:6, 8). Individuals, by themselves and in society, are creatures of flesh and blood, engaged in work as well as in worship. The God of the Psalter is concerned with the whole person and with the total society. Christians need to ask themselves how they may integrate this healthy sounding message with the dominant otherworldliness of the New Testament and traditional Christianity, and with the urban cocoon that shields them from the world of nature. Acts 14:17 and 1 Tim 6:17 are worth looking up in this connection. They are indications that the message of the Psalter is not to be forgotten.

6   SALVATION

If the theology of the orientation psalms is a theology of blessing, the theology of the psalms of disorientation and reorientation has in view a God who saves. A negative role of blessing is to keep misfortune at bay. When misfortune does strike, the divine activity to which appeal is made is that of salvation. Interest in the steady maintenance of life is replaced by a new concern, for sheer survival. There is an obvious tension here, which prompts the question why blessing is unable to do a perfect work, why it lets the serene "forever" of orientation be replaced by the poignant "how long?" of disorientation. To pose the question is to recall that "why?" is the question which in the lament preoccupies an anguished victim and ties him to his past in unhelpful regret. The fact that it does not find a regular answer sounds a warning: to ask our texts this question from an intellectual perspective is futile. It is enough to know that there were beneficent resources in the religion of the temple and in the Psalter, ready to be set in motion when crisis invaded life. The theology of the Psalms is pastoral rather than theoretical.

"Save me!" is the regular cry of the sufferer to God, for example in 3:7; 6:4, and 69:1. Similarly, in the communal lament of Ps 80 a plea for his intervention, "that we may be saved!" is the recurring refrain (vv 3, 7, 19 RSV). It is a child's instinctive clutching in time of sudden danger at the sleeve of a trusted adult. It acknowledges that the crisis is beyond one's own . capabilities, God-given though they are. A graphic illustration of this truth appears in the rescue of the shipwrecked mariners in Ps 107: "All their expertise [is] wrecked" (v 27). It is this element that characterizes disorientation and triggers off the mechanism of prayer.

1. *A biblical truth.* The Christian may be so influenced by systematic and evangelical theology and indeed by New Testament texts concerning salvation that he or she is embarrassed by the existential nature of the concept so prevalent in the laments. Is not religious salvation humanity's true need? Such embarrassment may reflect a stoical unwillingness to relate personal faith to the stark realities of human life—and so to the divine resources for meeting them. It is good to recall a factor that is generally overlooked, that the New Testament remained true to this dimension of salvation, at times freely applying its vocabulary to personal crisis.

In line with Ps 107, Acts 27:31 speaks of being "saved" from shipwreck; v 24 indicates that a theological perspective is not absent. In 2 Cor 1:10 St. Paul discusses in a blatantly theological way his being "delivered" from some unspecified crisis, perhaps sickness or physical assault. James 5:15 (RSV) declares that intercessory prayer "will save the sick man." These texts show an alertness to human crisis and a turning to God in the tradition of the Psalter. 2 Tim 4:17 (RSV) describes the outcome of the preliminary hearing of Paul's trial as being "rescued from the lion's mouth," in apparent reference to the petition of Ps 22:21. Presumably he had utilized the lament section of Ps 22 in prayer before and during the hearing. After the favorable outcome of the hearing he transformed the petition into an element of thanksgiving, namely the report of God's intervention.

2. *Images of crisis.* The lament tends to describe the crisis not in terms of particular and variable personal experiences but with standard images that highlight its destructive power and the emotional wounds it has inflicted. Even the general term *distress* or *trouble* is a conscious metaphor in those places where it is contrasted with the "wideness" of reorientation. "You knew about the distress of my soul. . . . you set my feet in a broad place" exclaims the psalmist in an affirmation of trust (31:7, 8). Other cases may be found in 4:1; 18:6, 19; 25:17, and 118:5. "Distress" literally means "narrowness" and reflects a situation of being cramped or pushed into a tight corner so that one is unable to realize life's potential. It is no accident that the English expressions *stress, distress, anguish,* and *straits* have also developed from the same basic meaning. They all reflect the human experience of unnatural confinement.

A similar metaphor, very widespread in the Psalter, is that of the trap, net, or pit which robs the victim of the human right of freedom. It may be found, for instance in 25:15; 31:4, and 116:3. Other metaphors abound, expressing disorientation in terms of negative sensations:

- it is darkness (18:28; 143:3).
- it is drowning in deep water (18:16; 69:1, 2, 15; 124:4, 5).
- it is a living death, depriving human existence of any intrinsic quality.

This image pervades Ps 88 and expresses so well its depth of anguish. A metaphor that may reflect the over-reacting characteristic of deep depression is the nightmarish portrayal of enemies as wild animals in Ps 22 (cf. 57:4). In the description of crisis at vv 12, 13, 16 the psalmist feels himself surrounded by bulls, lions, and dogs. The same obsessive images reappear in reverse order in the main passage of petition: "dog," "lion," and "wild oxen" (vv 20, 21).

3. *God's transforming power.* These multiple images of chaos serve to express the intolerable and excruciating nature of disorientation. In retrospect they also have the function of enhancing by contrast the subsequent reorientation. As already noted, the confinement of distress gives way to being at large and having room to move: to experience God's deliverance is to be "led . . . out to the broad place" (18:19). Likewise, God dispels the darkness by "light[ing] my lamp" (18:28). The factor that brings about reorientation is so essentially divine that "the Lord is my light" (27:1). He it is who breaks the snare and lets the bird flutter to freedom (124:6, 7). He is the rescuer who saves from drowning (18:16). He gives a new lease on life, terminating a living death and bringing up its victim from a veritable Sheol (30:3). Each negative image gives way to a positive counterpart, not by a natural swing of fortune but by a divine intervention that is a response to human prayer. This is the dynamic faith of the psalmists. They dared to believe that human distress was God's concern and that he was ready to stoop into disoriented lives and "[raise] the needy high above affliction" (107:41).

Salvation and covenant

While the phase of orientation is interpreted in the Psalter as under the control of the universal God of creation, the phase of reorientation is not viewed as a divine response to humanity as such. Deliverance is the privilege of the people of God. It operates within the circle of the covenant. "I am indeed your servant" and that is why "you have loosed my fetters," affirms the psalmist in thanksgiving (116:16). Because he was a true member of the community of faith, the faithful Lord of the covenant intervened on his behalf. The prayers of disorientation also find it necessary to refer to this factor as a condition of salvation, which they claim to meet.

1. *Two types of psalm.* This covenant perspective helps explain the double attitude to human sinning encountered in the laments, which Christians have found disconcerting. Sometimes sinning is acknowledged as the cause of crisis— but at other times this is firmly denied. Christian tradition has selected seven psalms as the "Penitential Psalms": Pss 6, 32, 38, 51, 102, 130, and 143. Most of them explicitly include confession of sins or allusions to sinning. Consequently it is often regarded as less significant that a number of other psalms appeal to integrity of life. Far from groveling before God, their demeanor is of one who approaches him "like a prince," to use Job's words in Job 31:37.

If these psalms are taken seriously, it is not difficult to relate them to a Christian framework of theology by dismissing them as sub-Christian, and to discard them as "Jewish" attempts to be justified by works. Such treatment is reminiscent of the reaction of certain Christians who would jettison the Sermon on the Mount as legalistic. The seizing upon certain psalms as normative for Christian usage and the virtual decanonizing of the contrary group betray an unwillingness to enter the theological world of the Psalter and to recognize that both types of psalm stem from a common covenant perspective.

2. *The randomness of crisis.* A factor that helps explain the double reaction to crisis in the laments, and which may be discussed first, is the existential nature of the distress which occasioned them. There is a randomness about human misfortune which makes it seem so unfair and prompts the perplexed question why? Why is my loved one struck down with cancer, while my neighbor's spouse stays in the pink of health? Why has my marriage broken down, while my neighbors continue to enjoy married bliss? Why did I lose my job, while my neighbor still draws a good salary? Why

has my boy landed in prison, while my neighbor's is a model citizen? Why have I suffered a nervous breakdown, while my neighbor handles stress with ease? Such a litany of modern woes corresponds to the situation of distress underlying the laments of the Psalter.

There is no standard answer to these questions, as the response of Jesus to the disciples' question—"who sinned, this man or his parents . . . ?" (John 9:2)—serves to acknowledge. Obviously many factors, knowable and unknowable, have contributed to such situations, and personal responsibility is a relevant factor to varying degrees or not at all. It would be foolish to conclude automatically, "It is because I'm a sinner that this misfortune has befallen me." Yet an objective analysis of the situation leading up to a particular crisis might prove incriminating for its victim and disclose that serious wrong on his or her part was responsible to a large degree. On the other hand, it might reveal that no particular blame could be laid at the victim's door.

The variability of these responses applies to the laments and songs of thanksgiving. It is significant that in Ps 107 two of the four cases of averted crisis are explicitly grounded in human reprehensibility (vv 11, 17), while the other two are eloquently silent on this point. The lament speakers search their consciences and are sometimes able to discern why they, rather than their neighbors, are suffering. Others can think of no such wrongs—unless, as Job grumbled, one rakes up some forgotten misdemeanors from the remote past (Job 13:26).

3. *God's part in human crisis.* In the case of Job and the psalmists it is necessary to observe that a strong factor of divine providence was understood to be present in the human situation. There was an act of God, in a theological sense. Thus an experience of social harassment was not adequately explained by human causation: "You deposited me in death's dust," it could be said of God (Ps 22:15).

Christians praying in time of crisis find themselves talking in these same terms. I can well remember as an eleven-year-old boy, minutes after being told of my mother's death, pounding the pillow with my fist and demanding, "Why did you have to let her die?" The psalmist too believed that God's providential activity lay at the root of human crisis. This factor at times increased the victim's perplexity, but his divine involvement was not doubted.

Disorientation meant to experience the wrath of God. It is important to grasp that this divine attribute or activity does not necessarily have a retributive role. If the victim is conscience-stricken in the sense described above, then it clearly does. But of itself it characterizes God in an alien role and constitutes an amoral, violent force beyond human control. It is so used in 6:1:

> O Lord, do not rebuke me in your anger
> and do not chastise me in your wrath.

Craigie rightly commented that "there is no confession of sin and there is no explicit statement of penitence."[16] Psalm 102 is another lament that mentions God's wrath in amoral terms:

> Ashes I eat for my food,
> with my drink I mingle tears
> because of your anger and wrath. . . . (vv 10, 11)

The inclusion of both laments in the Penitential Psalms is a result of jumping to conclusions about divine wrath. In Ps 88 the question why Yahweh has cast off the victim and hidden his face from him (v 14) is not answered by the reference to his destructive wrath in v 16, which serves rather to illustrate the severity of God's rejection. Similarly, the question in 74:1, "Why does thy anger smoke against the sheep of thy pasture?" is not intended as self-evident, but presents an attitude of utter perplexity.

Yet in a psalm which features confession of sin, wrath clearly has a retributive role. One example is 38:1–5:

> O Lord, do not rebuke me in your wrath. . . .
> My flesh has no soundness because of your indignation
> and my bones have no health because of my sin.

Ps 85:2, 3 is worth looking up and comparing. God is the referee who imposes penalties for infringement of the rules. The game of life has to be played according to the rules, which for Israel were laid down in its covenant traditions. In a situation of crisis the plea that comes readily to the psalmists' lips flows from a relationship with God by virtue of the covenant. However, when sin is admitted, the relationship becomes complex. God's self-imposed tasks in the covenant, like those of a parent in relation to his family, are twofold, to look after individual members of the covenant family and to maintain harmony by discipline. What unifies the two tasks is the promotion of the ultimate interests of family members. Even if a son or daughter has committed an offense against the ethos of the family, he or she is still a member of the family. As the disrupter, he or she is expected to apologize and seek to restore the harmony befitting the relationship.

This kind of family relationship pervades those laments that include confession of sin, such as Pss 25, 32, 38, 39, and 79. Ps 32 is a song of thanksgiving that looks back to a crisis that represented fair punishment. It draws from the experience the general lesson that every "godly" person should pray at such a time and would find forgiveness and help from God. The Hebrew word for "godly," *hasid*, refers to one who is on the receiving end of God's *hesed*, steadfast love or covenant loyalty, as a member of the covenant circle. Ps 25 likewise pleads God's steadfast love (v 6). Forgiveness is sought "for your name's sake" (v 11), that is, so that God may thus be true to his self-revelation as the covenant God who desires harmony. Ps 79, a communal lament, pleads at the outset that, sinners though they are, they are also within the circle of the covenant: they are "thy saints"—the same Hebrew term as is used for "godly" in 32:6—and "thy servants" (79:2).

4. *Human and divine "righteousness."* In the chapter on faith it was observed that the vocative phrase "my God" dominates the psalms of lament. This is another version of the claim to a joint relationship. Yet another is the appeal to God's "righteousness." In 5:7, 8 mention of his righteousness and his "lovingkindness" ("steadfast love," RSV) occur almost in the same breath and are obviously poetic variants. Righteousness basically means conformity to a norm. In this case the norm is the covenant. Righteousness is not here a moral attribute, but connotes acting in a manner consistent with covenant commitment and doing the right thing in the light of it. The reader can look up other cases of this specialized sense of the term in 35:24 and 71:2. In 143:1 it is paralleled with God's faithfulness. Yahweh is "righteous" (RSV), celebrates 129:4 in tones of thanksgiving: he is loyal to the obligations he has voluntarily undertaken in the covenant.

Appeal to covenant membership is understandably present in laments which can find no retributive force in their particular experience of crisis. As observed above, crisis is no respecter of persons, and does not match moral culpability. It is hardly surprising that a number of psalms make this point: Pss 7, 11, 17, 18, and 139.

As for Ps 139, its treatment of the omniscience and omnipresence of God in terms of praise is no theological idyll. Its final verses reveal that it is grounded in the hurly-burly of the game of life. It appeals to the divine referee to take the psalmist's side against accusations of foul play. "Examine me, O God, and know my mind" (v 23) is an invitation based upon a belief in personal innocence. With the same mingled tones of praise and protest the apostle Paul affirmed in 2 Cor 11:31 (RSV): "The God and Father of the Lord Jesus, he who is blessed for ever, knows that I do not lie."

Pss 7 and 17 move in a similar orbit of false accusation. Ps 18, a royal thanksgiving for military victory, dwells at length on personal "righteousness," that is, a general consistency with the obligations of the covenant (vv 20–24). It goes on to draw out the truth that, when crisis comes, God honors such consistency with deliverance:

> With the faithful, you show yourself faithful;
> with the blameless, you show yourself blameless.
> With the pure, you show yourself pure,
> and with the twisted, you deal tortuously. . . .
> He is a shield for all who seek refuge in him. (vv 25–30)

There is here no theological statement of moral perfection, but the emphatic expression of a lesser claim of not being a backslider, to use a Christian term. Nor is there considered to be any manifestation of pride; humility, rather than self-righteous pride, is professed:

> For thou dost deliver a humble people;
> but the haughty eyes thou dost bring down. (v 27, RSV)

The point is that the attack from the king's national enemies had not simultaneously functioned as a divine judgment for apostasy. It was not unreasonable, therefore, that Yahweh should have come powerfully to the aid of his covenant partner, with no reservations. Yet this aid is not taken for granted, but, once given, becomes the object of enthusiastic, grateful praise, in vv 1–3 and 31–50.

Ps 11, a lament-related composition, makes the same point from a stage further back. It honestly claims that its crisis is of the nonpunitive type. So there is no ambivalence in the divine-human relationship, and an appeal for God to protect his own is an uncomplicated matter. Here again there is no manifestation of pride. Rather, the psalmist throws himself upon God as the object of his trust: "In the Lord I have sought refuge" (v 1). Similar comment might be made about Ps 44, a communal lament which robustly professes loyalty to God (vv 17–21) and significantly concludes with appeal to God's own unchanging loyalty, his steadfast love, or "lovingkindness":

Arise! Help us!
And redeem us because of your lovingkindness. (v 26)

Overall, the Psalter appears to be saying that God honors his own, but that "backsliding" constitutes a complication that has to be dealt with before covenant aid can be received. Essentially the expectation of receiving it is grounded not in human self-confidence but in the faithfulness of the God of the covenant.

Salvation as a theological heritage

It is obvious that when the psalmist pleads, "save me," the term is not being used in the evangelistic sense in which it was used of Cornelius in Acts 11:14. The psalmist already moved within the active orbit of God's covenant relationship with Israel, entered by birth and made his own by faith, as 22:10 and 71:6 affirm. Yet there is in the Psalms a looking back to God's archetypal work of salvation.

1. *Sacred history.* In the communal laments a standard element is the harking back to the saving work performed by Yahweh at the outset of Israel's covenant history. A notable instance is 74:2, where God is urged to act in a manner consistent with his initial acquisition and redemption of the community of faith at the Exodus:

Remember thy congregation, which thou hast
gotten of old,
which thou hast redeemed to be the tribe of
thy heritage! (RSV)

The appeal seems to echo Exod 15:13, 16 or a similar tradition. In the same way a song of thanksgiving appears to
declare that Exod 15:2 has become true again in recent
experience: "Yah(weh) is my strength and protection; he has
become my savior" (118:14). Craigie has suggested that
there is an allusion to Exod 15:11–13, an individual lament,
in 17:7:

Reveal the wonder of your lovingkindness,
you who deliver by your right hand
those seeking refuge from assailants.[17]

To return to the communal lament, 44:1–3 celebrates "our
fathers[']" occupation of Canaan by God's enabling. So too
does Ps 80 under the allegory of a vine in vv 8, 9:

Thou didst bring a vine out of Egypt . . . .
It took deep root and filled the land. (RSV)

In both these cases past salvation serves as a model of hope
for present deliverance.
2. *Contemporary relevance.* God's salvation of "our fathers" is described in 22:3–5 as a theme of Israel's hymnic
praises. Ps 105 might be cited as such a hymn. It exults in
Israel's present enjoyment of a heritage that stretches back
to the patriarchs, with whom Israel's foundations as God's
chosen people were laid. Ps 114 presents an imaginative
treatment of the Exodus and occupation of Canaan, which
transports worshipers back to the scene, making them feel as
if it were all just happening. Israel's origins in theological

history are relevant as the basis of their contemporary self-understanding.

Another dramatic characterization of history is the description of the crossing of the Red Sea in the hymnic passage of a lament-related composition, 77:11–20. Seemingly the psalmist's sufferings were bound up with those of God's people. Both personal and communal hope was found in looking back to their ancient history as proof that "Thou art the God who workest wonders" (v 14 RSV). Yahweh's power once prevailed over the waters of chaos which could have overwhelmed Israel, killing it at birth. So there was hope that present chaos would meet its match in God.

Verses 10–24 of Ps 136 present in a hymn the sacred events from Egypt to Canaan in terms of their once-for-all significance as a guarantee of God's perpetual "steadfast love." In vv 23, 24 the theme of the Exodus is evidently treated again, now with a contemporary nuance: Yahweh remembered "us" when we suffered in Egypt and rescued "us." In principle we were there participating in that salvation, declares Israel, and we still now enjoy its benefits.

3. *Christian echoes.* In the New Testament the death and resurrection of Jesus stand out as basic saving events to which the church looks back as the once-for-all work of God and as the ground of its self-understanding. We can now appreciate that in one sense there is nothing new about such an interpretation. The New Testament has picked up a cue provided in the Old, which already recognized certain events in human history to be of crucial theological significance. The memory of them stayed green in the praises of every generation of God's people. In Christ God has acted in a manner consistent with his former revelation, so that the proclamation of his new work spells "the power of God for salvation" (Rom 1:16 RSV).

Hope is faith with its face turned to the future. Several examples of the vocabulary of faith given in the fourth chapter would fit equally well at this point. The overlap of faith and hope may be illustrated from their terms being placed together in parallelism, as in 71:5:

> For thou, O Lord, art my hope,
> my trust, O Lord, from my youth. (RSV)

Other examples of this tendency may be found in 25:20, 21; 33:18, 20; 146:5; 147:11. Faith is essentially a commitment to God and to his protective power not only in the present but also for the future.

Grounds for hope

1. *God's covenant.* The basis of assurance for a future better than the present is the relationship established by God with his people. Occasionally the substance of hope is

encapsulated in a categorical statement, an assertion which affirms this covenant basis for hope. A clear instance is at 94:14 in the course of a lament. The tide of disorientation will eventually turn

> For the Lord will not forsake his people;
> he will not abandon his heritage. . . . (RSV)

In 9:18 a more oblique assurance is given:

> The poor will not always be forgotten
> nor will the hope of the afflicted perish forever.

The context makes plain that "the ones who know your name" (v 10) are in view and that Yahweh is the implicit agent, remembering his own. The roots of this covenant relationship in theological history are the theme of Ps 78. The psalm teaches a lesson in religious education, with the aim that the next generation

> should set their hope in God and not forget the
> works of God,
> but keep his commandments. . . . (v 7 RSV)

One might render that verse "set their confidence in God": the line between faith and hope is very tenuous here. In favor of the Revised Standard Version's translation is the parallelism of a closely related term with a word which definitely denotes hope in the Hebrew of Job 4:6. Hope is envisaged as a commitment of the whole life to God. It entails the adoption of a lifestyle that matches the traditions of the covenant. Yahweh is to be the target of human existence.

This hope essentially depends upon an understanding of the historical era from Moses to David as the focus of God's revelation of himself to "our fathers" (78:5). This understanding was passed down from generation to generation as the basis of Israel's self-understanding. An arc is traced from "our fathers" to "children yet unborn" (v 6): the future of the people of God is rooted in the past.

2. *God's steadfast love.* Since the covenant involved not only commitment to God but God's commitment to his people, it is not surprising that the covenant attribute of his unchanging loyalty is presented as the source of Israel's hope. Twice in the Psalter God's people are designated as those who "hope in his steadfast love" or "lovingkindness" (33:18; 147:11). In both cases the nuance of the Hebrew term *hesed* is his habitual provision of deliverance to members of his community whenever they are in need. Yahweh comes to the rescue of his own as their faithful ally. Ps 33 rises to a climax in the petitionary wish, "May your loving kindness be upon us, O Lord, as we have depended on you" (v 22).

There is a personal laying hold of the general statement of v 18 cited above. The praising community acknowledge themselves to be in the role described there and turn theology into prayer. A perusal of this hymn discloses the pervasiveness of steadfast love: it is celebrated in vv 5, 18 and 22. As Lord of creation and Lord of the covenant, Yahweh is equally characterized by the quality of steadfast love. Indeed, the term permeates the Psalter and makes it the book of God's grace. The reader of this book may have noticed how, in reflection of this phenomenon, this particular divine virtue has found its way into every chapter thus far. Seemingly one cannot keep it out of a discussion of any aspect of the Psalms.[18] Here it is God's readiness to help his own, without which they cannot face the future.

Ps 138, a song of thanksgiving, gives a further example of this attitude of hope. In v 2 the grateful mention of steadfast love refers to specific deliverance, as it does in the thanksgiving formula, "Give thanks to Yahweh, for . . . his steadfast love is everlasting." The actual formula is reflected in v 8:

Yahweh, your loyal love is everlasting.
Do not abandon the product of your hands.

Although no vocabulary of hope is present, clearly here is one who hopes in Yahweh's steadfast love. The renewal of his previous experience of God's saving help, celebrated in v 2, may not be taken for granted. There has to be a petition for it to be manifested afresh whenever necessary in the precarious course of human life.

In Ps 100 there is a similar movement from past and present to the future on the basis of God's steadfast love. In this case, although the thank-offering service seems to have been the original setting of the psalm, as the heading indicates, it is nevertheless a hymn and so widens the perspective of steadfast love from specific thanksgiving to general praise. It is an attribute which marks Yahweh's habitual relationship to his people. In v 5 the note of permanence latent in the Hebrew term and expressed in the thanksgiving formula is pressed into service as a feature of the covenant relationship:

> For the Lord is good:
> his steadfast love endures for ever,
> and his faithfulness to all generations. (RSV)

The reasons for praise began in v 3 by celebrating God's past creation of Israel as his people. It is a truth of contemporary validity: "It is he that made us, and we are his." Verse 5 moves forward to a reassuring declaration of the future implications of this basic fact for "all generations," because of his steadfast love.

The classic statement of this divine basis for human hope is to be found outside the Psalter, in Lam 3:22–24. The victim of Jerusalem's destruction testifies that he "will hope in" God because of the everlasting nature of his steadfast love, which is "new every morning." As for the Psalms, this relation between steadfast love and hope is given unequivocal expression in 130:7, 8:

> Put your hope, Israel, in Yahweh,
> for with Yahweh there is loyal love
> and redemption with him in abundance,
> and he it is who will redeem Israel
> from all their iniquities.

Redemption took its theological cue from God's work at the Exodus, but it found ample confirmation in God's treatment of his people since then. Here it is aligned with steadfast love, as it is also in Deut 7:8, 9. Confession is made that present adversity is the result of sinning, but the community is urged to take seriously as a pointer to their future a deduction from the oft-revealed character of God. Not condemnation but deliverance is to be their lot. The argument from past to present and future on the basis of the formula "his steadfast love endures forever" also seems to underlie a Song of Zion, Ps 48:

> We have thought on thy steadfast love, O God,
> in the midst of thy temple. . . .
> this is God, our God for ever and ever.
> He will be our guide for ever. (vv 9, 14 RSV)

Again this is a motif of hope, although the specific vocabulary of hope is not employed.

3. *God's majesty unchangingness.* The "foreverness" of God is also presented as a hope motif in 102:12–22 and 123:1, 2 (see also 92:7, 8 and 135:13, 14). In Ps 102 a reversal of Israel's grim fortunes is expected in the future. The ground of this expectation is his heavenly kingship above the time-bound earth: Yahweh is "enthroned forever"

(v 13). Verses 25–28 present similar reasons why Israel may hope in a positive future. The divine king of creation is immortal, and he is immune from the obsolescence that marks his creation: "You are the same, and your years do not end." Because he lives, there is hope that his people too will live.

In 123:1, 2 the language of hope is used in conjunction with the truth of God's supernatural kingship. When the suffering community keeps on looking to Yahweh "till" he comes to their aid, the object of their hoping gaze is one who is "enthroned in the heavens."

Existential hope

1. *Hope during crisis.* Like a rope thrown to a drowning person, the hope of the Psalter is effective amid the harsh realities of human existence. Whenever the lamenter wearily asked God "How long?" there was a stirring of hope. What kept the victims of disorientation going was the consciousness of a higher reality which encouraged them to daringly envisage positive life beyond their present living death. "And now, what have I hoped for, O Lord? My hope is for you!" is the sufferer's question and answer in 39:7. The trusting declaration of 62:1 has a similar emphasis:

> For God alone my soul waits in silence;
> from him comes my salvation. (RSV)

Ps 119 gives this basic statement a characteristic twist when repeatedly in its setting of distress it makes the Torah, which represents God, the focus of hope: "I put my hope in your word" (v 114, see also vv 43, 49, 74, 81, 147, 166).

The eyes are the physical organs metaphorically associated with hope. They look up to God in heaven, awaiting his championship of his oppressed servants (123:1, 2).

Sometimes they grow tired and sore, waiting for a deliverance that seems never to come:

> My eyes grow dim
> with waiting for my God. (69:3 RSV)

Yet still one waits—"I have waited for you all the day long" (25:5)—clinging to a conviction that God is bound to intervene eventually:

> For the poor will not always be forgotten,
> nor will the hope of the afflicted perish forever. (9:18)

When famine strikes or death threatens from another quarter, hope in God is all that can see its victims through the crisis:

> Lo, the Lord's eye is upon those that fear him,
> upon those that depend on his loving kindness,
> to rescue their soul from death
> and to keep them alive in famine. (33:18, 19)

This God-centered hope gave to sufferers a morale which would otherwise have been completely lacking. The refrain of Pss 42/43 places on record a mental dialogue that keeps utter despair at bay:

> O my soul, why are you downcast
> and so disturbed within me?
> Wait patiently for God, for I will praise him again. . . .
> (42:5, 11; 43:5)

The references to God's eventual intervention as the ground of praise are like the noticing of milestones along the road, which remind the weary traveler of his hoped-for destination and encourage him to plod on prayerfully.

Yet, as the third chapter observed, although the praise of the thanksgiving song is necessarily absent from the lament, the lament does know its own praise. It is grounded in previous experience of God and in his known character. At 71:14, in the light of v 8, this type of praise is also an expression of hope, which defiantly counters the catcalls of persecutors:

> But I will hope continually
> and will praise thee yet more and more. (RSV)

The religious phenomenon awaited by the suffering psalmist was a divine oracle of response:

> I have waited for you, O Lord;
> you will answer, O Lord my God. (38:15)

This waiting for a ruling from the sanctuary is described as a desire more ardent than that of "watchmen for the morning" (130:5, 6). The comparison is an apt one: the sufferer knew an experience of darkness and an onslaught of danger that affected him even more intensely than the potential perils of the night troubled the sentries peering from the town's watchtower.

2. *Hope in God's word of promise.* Even when the divine word did come, the need to hope was not removed. Ps 27:14 appears to be an official message, implicitly assuring that God would intervene on the psalmist's behalf, but urging confident morale during the time lag between this promise and its fulfillment:

> Wait for the Lord! Be strong,
> and let your heart be bold.
> Yes, wait for the Lord.

Hovering between disorientation and reorientation, one psalmist responds to a favorable oracle not only with praise to God but also with encouragement to others who still waited for good news:

> Be strong and take heart,
> all you who are waiting on the Lord. (31:24)

The one who has been helped turns into a helper of others. There is a beautiful pastoral concern here. It is also evident in 22:26:

> The afflicted shall eat and shall be satisfied;
> those who seek him shall praise the Lord—
> may your hearts live forever!

It is probable too that the exhortation in 130:7, "Put your hope, Israel, in Yahweh," originally represented a sequel to the receipt of the divine word awaited in v 5. The person to whom deliverance has been promised can testify to a needy community from the higher vantage point he has reached in his personal pilgrimage.

From a still higher position the thanksgiving song bears witness to the full experience of salvation as the attaining of one's hopes:

> I waited patiently for the Lord,
> and he turned to me and heard my cry.
> And he raised me from the pit of desolation,
> from the slimy mud,
> and he set my feet upon a rock;
> and he made firm my footsteps. (40:1, 2)

Again the context refers to a pastoral expectation that others will be encouraged in their faith by his testimony:

> Many will see and will fear,
> and they will trust in the Lord. (v 3)

Answered prayer confers an uplifting ministry.

3. *Hope for life's continuance.* Hope, like faith, blossoms best in the phase of disorientation, according to the Psalter. But it would be false to conclude that the phase of orientation knows nothing of hope. Eschatological hope will be discussed a little later, but the believer's hoping trust in God as a regular phenomenon also finds a place in the Psalms. Mention of 78:7 has been made earlier; comparable is 71:5:

> For thou, O Lord, art my hope,
> my trust, O Lord, from my youth. (RSV)

A. A. Anderson has aptly compared the promise of God-given orientation in Jer 29:11 (RSV), "I know the plans I have for you, says the Lord, plans . . . to give you a future and a hope."[19] There is a projection of this covenantal hope upon the larger screen of creation in 104:27 (and probably thence in 145:15). Animate creatures are perceived as a family of God's dependents, trusting him for their daily supply of food: "In hope all of them look to you." This imaginative perspective—also evident in the portrayal of lions at prayer in v 21!—vividly communicates what elsewhere in the Bible is expressed objectively rather than subjectively: it is only God's upholding that keeps the world in continued existence. The vivid language of 104:27 appears to underlie the eschatological hope ascribed to creation in Rom 8:19, "the creation waits with eager longing. . . ." There the motif is interestingly linked with prophetic language of disorientation in v 22; Isa 21:3 may be fruitfully compared.

The Psalter has its own brand of eschatological hope in the sense of expecting an epoch-making divine intervention which would inaugurate the fulfillment of Israel's earthly destiny. Von Rad's characterization of the Old Testament as a piece of literature of constantly growing but never fulfilled expectation[20] may require some refinement, but insofar as it is true it includes the Psalter, where hope of an eschatological kind is concerned. Israel already knew the Christian affirmations that "in . . . hope we were saved" and that for this hope "we wait . . . with patience" (Rom 8:24, 25). In Ps 37, a wisdom psalm, the ancient motif of inheriting the land is projected forward and given afresh as an ultimate hope to those who "wait for the Lord" and obey him (v 34). Verses 3, 9, 11, 22, 29 illustrate the pervasiveness of this motif in the psalm, to which appeal is made as a longed-for ideal. An old understanding of Israel's destiny as heirs of the land is reemployed.

This also happens in 125:3:

> The scepter of wickedness
> will surely not remain
> over the land allotted to the righteous,
> or else the righteous might turn
> their hands to wrongdoing.

Here the hope is pressed into the service of wisdom's ethical concerns as an incentive to perseverance in well doing.

1. *God's character.* Eschatological hope is grounded in God's own being. In 86:8, 9 it is because of Yahweh's uniqueness that universal worship at Jerusalem is a future certainty:

> There is none like thee among the gods, O Lord,
> nor are there any works like thine.

All the nations thou hast made shall come
and bow down before thee, O Lord,
and shall glorify thy name. (RSV)

In 102:13–22 the citation of prophetic hopes that
Jerusalem would be restored as a religious center of universal
homage is founded solidly upon the truth of Yahweh's everlasting kingship, as a direct and logical corollary (see too
vv 25–28; also see 69:6, 34–36). Yahweh's role as king must
involve his eventual intervention to set the world to rights:

Let the hills sing for joy together
before the Lord, for he comes
to judge the earth.
He will judge the world with righteousness,
and the peoples with equity. (98:8, 9 RSV; cf. 96:10–13)

It was the nature of God that dictated and guaranteed
Israel's future hope. Not "that" but "when" was the only
uncertainty:

Remember me, Yahweh, when you show your people favor,
notice me when you save them. (106:4)

God's self-grounded promise was a time bomb of latent energy, ticking away until its set time should come.
2. *God's purposes for his people.* Israel's conviction of a
divine purposefulness meant that "he who began a good
work in you will bring it to completion . . ." (Phil 1:6). It is
to this God, who does not leave things half finished, that
prayer is addressed in the post-exilic Ps 126. Earlier he had
been experienced as one who "restored Zion's fortunes"
(v 1). The return from exile was the inauguration of prophetic promises, with which the phrase "restore fortunes"
is mainly associated. Unfortunately the time of God's great

work (vv 2, 3) had given way to a period of small things (Zech 4:10). Yet the post-exilic community had known Yahweh as the saving, restoring God, as the fulfiller of psalmodic hopes (see 14:7) in addition to prophetic expectations. To such a God they brought their appeal that he repeat, and so fulfill, his saving activity: "Yahweh, restore our fortunes" (v 4).

3. *God's royal promises.* Ps 126 belongs to the Songs of Ascents, a self-contained collection which places no little stress on eschatological hope. Within the collection the exhortation to Israel in 130:7, 8 to maintain its hope, a hope grounded in God's steadfast love, assumes a forward-looking role; so too does the similar 131:3.

Both psalm endings prepare the way for an elaboration of Israel's hope in Ps 132, which is a royal psalm that cites divine warrant for the Davidic dynasty enthroned in Zion. In the post-exilic and so post-monarchical collection of the Songs of Ascents (Pss 120–134) this royal psalm obviously acquired meaning for the future, as indeed the fanfare of future expectation in the two preceding psalms clearly indicates. Ps 132 carries great weight in its present context. Of all the Songs of Ascents, it stands out as the longest composition. Its importance is also indicated by its climactic positioning near the end of the collection: Pss 133 and 134 necessarily close it with notes of benediction (133:3; 134:3). In the light of the collection's favorite theme, a key purpose of Ps 132 is to glorify Zion, the sacred place of pilgrimage. It is no accident that statements of Zion's role in Yahweh's purposes find firm mention in it (vv 13–17). The psalm adds a new dimension to Zion's destiny by stressing that the Davidic monarchy was to play a crucial part in it ("there," v 17). Accordingly a royal psalm became a focus of Israel's hopes for its future under God.

Much the same may be said of the role of the royal psalms to be found throughout the final form of the Psalter, as

Hope

Claus Westermann has observed.[21] It is reasonable to assume that originally the royal psalms comprised a single collection. If so, the dismembering process evident in the Korahite and Asaphite collections has been carried to extremes in this case. They are scattered throughout the total collection, as if at random. However, they seem to function like the fruit in a well-made cake, ensuring that with every slice of psalmody testimony to the royal hope is present. The strategic placing of certain royal psalms supports this interpretation. Just as Ps 132 had a climactic role near the end of the Songs of Ascents, so Books Two and Three significantly end with royal psalms, Pss 72 and 89.

The royal theme is obviously of prime importance in the redactional ordering of the Psalter: Ps 2, the first psalm after the introductory Ps 1, belongs to the royal collection and is probably a late pre-exilic specimen. Indeed, Westermann has suggested that at one stage there was a Torah-wisdom edition of the Psalter which began with Ps 1 and ended with Ps 119.[22] If so, Pss 2 and 118, both royal psalms, were given pride of place as the A and Z of the edition inside its Torah-wisdom wrappings.

The royal psalms were originally pre-exilic compositions. They attested the importance of the existing Davidic monarchy in the theological thinking of Israel and also in its institutional religion. It is characteristic of the Psalter to give new meaning to old material, and this feature finds a fresh manifestation in the royal psalms.

Although the monarchy ceased to be part of Israel's history at the end of the pre-exilic period, as Ps 89 tragically laments, it lived on as part of Israel's hope, substantiated by God's sworn word "forever" (89:1–4, 28–37). In the context of the canonical Psalter the import of this psalm shifts from pleading lament to praise of God's dynastic promises, in defiance of ongoing world history. The editorial doxology of 89:52 is justified! Already in the late shaping of the Psalter

what might with reservations be called a messianic significance has been attached to these royal psalms. History has
become eschatology. The New Testament's novel interpretation is not that it gives the royal psalms a messianic role,
since that is nothing new, but that it relates them to the
person and work of Jesus as the Christ and proclaims
the presence of Israel's king and the dawn of its eschatological hope.

8 SCRIPTURE

At first sight the presence of the book of Psalms in the scripture canon of Judaism and Christianity is astonishing. How elastic the concept of scripture must have been to regard what are obviously human words as divine revelation! Essentially the Psalter constitutes a response to God in prayer and praise. However, by New Testament times the authority of the Psalms is not the existential authority of believers who have lived through good times and bad, and left on record their impressions for posterity to benefit from. The authority of the Psalter is much higher: no less a biblical formula than "as it is written" introduces a chain of psalm references in Rom 3:10 and 15:9. In Heb 1:7 the statement of Ps 104:4, indubitably human in the light of v 1, is presented as God's words ("he says"). Likewise, in Heb 1:8, 9 the extravaganza of the court poet in honor of a royal wedding (Ps 45:6, 7) is graced with the same formula. The implied presupposition has already been made plain in Heb 1:1: as part of the Old Testament, the Psalms have a place in God's inspired communication to Israel. Such an accolade deserves some explanation. Let us try to recover the process whereby human words became acknowledged as vehicles of divine truth.

The authority of the Psalms

A key factor is the Psalter's function as temple literature. In pre-exilic and post-exilic history the temple was an institution that mediated Yahweh to his people.

1. *Priestly and prophetic contributions.* The personnel of the temple were invested with authority as his mouthpieces. The prophetic liturgies bear clear witness to this phenomenon: God's prophets delivered divine oracles, which they introduced in their own persons before using the divine "I": "I hear a voice I had not known" (81:5, 6–16) and "O that today you would listen to his voice!" (95:7, 8–11).

The prophetic introduction in 85:8, "Let me hear what God the Lord will speak" (RSV), is followed by a third-person exposition of the divine message of "peace" (vv 9–13). The royal Ps 132 consists not only of the king's prayer but also of answering assurances that are grounded in Yahweh's oracles concerning Zion and the role of the monarchy in his purposes for Zion (vv 11, 12, 14–18). Other royal psalms cite divine oracles, namely 2:7–9 and 110:1, 4. Interestingly it is this prophetic element to which the Letter to the Hebrews attaches not a little importance. Heb 1:5, 13; 5:5, 6; and 7:21 quote the oracles of Ps 2:7 and 110:4 as the statements of God himself. Heb 3:7–11 (cf. 4:3, 5, 7) cites the prophetic Ps 95:7–11 with a formula "as the Holy Spirit says." Not a little stress is laid on divine first-person language in the Psalms as the basis of the argument in Hebrews concerning the purposes of God.

A similar testimony to divineness in the Psalter is given by the contribution made by priests. There are priestly liturgies which relate to access to the temple courts and to departure from them. The entrance liturgy of Ps 15 mainly consists of a priestly response to a pilgrim's question (vv 2–5; cf. 24:3–6). The priest functioned as the spokesperson of God in presenting ethical standards. So he did when he bestowed benediction, for instance, in 121:3–7, in response to a worshiper's expression (vv 1, 2) of a need to have his faith strengthened:

> He will not let your foot stumble; . . .
> Yahweh will guard you
> from all danger,
> he will guard your life.

Ps 91 is similar. The text and perspective of vv 1, 2 are uncertain and may represent a pilgrim's own confession of faith, but vv 3–13 cannot be other than a priestly response, which is capped by a formal, divine oracle in vv 14–16:

> Because he cleaves to me in love, I will deliver him;
> I will protect him, because he knows my name.
> When he calls to me, I will answer him;
> I will be with him in trouble, . . . (RSV)

Such prophetic and priestly contributions to the Psalms claim divine authority. Significantly in both types God's revelation is given not only in first-person communications but also with third-person language. The way was thereby open to regarding other third-person pronouncements as invested with divine authority in this book that partook of the institutional character of the temple.

2. *The temple as a divine institution.* Judah after the Exile took seriously the divine role of the temple and listened carefully to the testimony of Ps 78 that with David and the building of the temple God had inaugurated a new era. The post-exilic community reveled in their participation in this temple era, as the books of Chronicles bear witness. The musical and choral organization went back to David and to

the prophetic authority of Gad and Nathan, and accordingly were inspired by God (2 Chr 29:25). The praises of Yahweh sung by the Levitical choirs used "the words of David and of Asaph the seer" (2 Chr 29:30). Again the prophetic ascription was intended to stamp the temple constitution as divine—in this case its psalmodic element. David was regarded as God's minister in setting up a system that reflected his will (cf. 1 Chr 15:16-24; 16:4-7, 41).

So, returning to the Psalter, it is not difficult to regard the choral collections of Asaph and the sons of Korah as expressions of God's own desire that he should be praised in this way. By a natural extension such an understanding was easily ascribed to psalms not explicitly associated with Levitical choirs, as they became part of the treasury of temple psalmody. In accord with this conception is the phenomenon observed in the third chapter, the role of the doxologies as responses to God's praiseworthiness elaborated in the preceding blocks of material. At this level the humanity of the Psalms was played down, while those elements that explicitly glorified God were highlighted. The doxologies regard human phenomena as trappings for this divine centrality. They turn the Psalms into affirmations about God and so serve to reinforce their authoritative nature.

3. *The authority of wisdom teaching.* There is another factor to be taken into account as a further step toward the canonization of the Psalter, whereby it gained binding authority for Israel's teaching about God. A number of modes of inspiration are reflected in the biblical literature, and the direct mode of the prophetic variety is by no means the only one. Wisdom literature had its own concept of divine authority. The wisdom teacher was a source of religious authority for Israel along with the prophet and the priest, according to Jer 18:18. Human observation, reflection, and discussion were channels through which divine inspiration came. The wisdom teacher spoke of his words as divinely authoritative:

For the Lord gives wisdom;
from his mouth come knowledge and understanding . . .
(Prov 2:6 RSV)

The descriptions of King Solomon, whom 1 Kings regarded as the sage *par excellence*, reflect this double perspective. Wisdom was credited to Solomon inasmuch as it was exercised by him, according to 1 Kgs 4:30, 34 and 10:4, 6–8—but primarily it was God's, for "all Israel . . . perceived that the wisdom of God was in him" (3:28 RSV). The divine stamp of wisdom teaching is relevant for the Psalms. The wisdom psalms, both those not composed for use in the temple and those which employed wisdom language with a temple setting in mind, must have brought into the Psalter their own religious authority.

4. *The Psalms as Torah.* In this connection the importance of Ps 1 as an introduction to the Psalter cannot be underestimated. If, as some scholars have urged, Pss 1 and 119 once framed an edition of the Psalter designed for a wisdom setting, then wisdom's authority was regarded as extending from Ps 2 to Ps 118. Be that as it may, the presence of Ps 1 served to invest the book of Psalms with a distinctive aura. In itself Ps 1 represents a late development of wisdom thinking which fused wisdom concerns with high regard for the Torah. In this context Torah is not to be understood as relating simply to the Pentateuch: it had gained a wider literary perspective.

In Ps 119 there seems to be literary dependence on Deuteronomy—and also on the books of Proverbs, Isaiah, and Jeremiah. Prophetic sources and wisdom material, as well as a pentateuchal book, were interpreted as Scriptures in which God had made known his character and his purposes for his people. In turn the function of Ps 1 appears to be to interpret the Psalms that follow as Torah or the written revelation of God.

The final verse of the book of Hosea is a wisdom postscript which casts wisdom's aura of authority over the prophetic book:

> Whoever is wise, let him understand these things;
> whoever is discerning, let him know them; . . .
>   (Hos 14:9 RSV)

Even more categorically, Ps 1 seems to identify the Psalter as Torah and to commend it from this perspective as the fitting object of the believer's absorbed meditation:

> In the Lord's Torah is his delight
> and in his Torah will he muse by day and night. (v 2)

This introductory statement about the Psalter made by Ps 1 is an extreme one, but it represents only further progress along the path trodden by the doxologies in characterizing the Psalms as God-centered compositions. Brevard S. Childs has rightly commented concerning this shift in understanding: "Because Israel continues to hear God's word through the voice of the psalmists' response, these prayers now function as the divine word itself."[23]

David as exemplar

Childs has also found canonical significance in the historicizing Davidic superscriptions, in that David was viewed as a representative person "who displays all the strengths and weaknesses of all human beings."[24]

1. *The Davidic superscriptions.* Thirteen psalms have headings which relate them to episodes in the life of David. Most of the superscriptions interpret enemies in their particular psalms as historical personages or groups who are mentioned in 1 and 2 Samuel: Saul (Pss 18, 54, 57, 59),

Absalom (Ps 3), an unknown Cush (Ps 7), Doeg the Edomite (Ps 52), the Philistines (Ps 56), and Abimelech in particular (Ps 34) and the Arameans (Ps 60).

Other headings give biographical identifications in topographical terms, in Pss 63 and 142, while a lament featuring confession of sin is linked with Bathsheba in the heading to Ps 51. There are good reasons for classifying most of these references as the result of a historicizing process similar to the "connective" type of midrashic exposition of the Psalms practiced by the rabbis.[25] Using linguistic and thematic analogies, they endeavored to connect individual psalms with personages and events in Old Testament history. The Greek version of the Psalms continues this hermeneutical process, linking further psalms with David and also with other historical characters and incidents.

What was the motivation behind the Davidic captions? Childs' interpretation of David as a typical human figure is impressive, but it has met with some scholarly dissent. Is not his "everyman" approach a contradiction of the concern for ancient history in these superscriptions? Does not the process represent rather a reductive, retrograde shift from leaving the Psalms open to use by anybody at any time toward an antiquarian exclusiveness? These criticisms are not unreasonable. If Childs is right, further argumentation is necessary to justify a leap from Davidic history to contemporary relevance.

2. *Role modeling in Chronicles.* Appeal to the Chronicler's theological approach to history may begin to build a bridge between past and present. In Chronicles the age of David and Solomon marks the start of a new era of grace which extends to the Chronicler's own time. It establishes positive criteria whereby the lives of subsequent generations may be judged. In general the planning and building of the temple provided a new key for explaining Israel's existence thereafter. David's generosity in his material provision for

the temple is presented as a model for Israel which the Chronicler surely intended his own generation to note (1 Chr 29:18). To Solomon are revealed God's principles of dealing with his people (2 Chr 7:14), which became the criterion for assessing future kings (see 2 Chr 36:11–16) and in particular, for explaining the eventual rehabilitation of Manasseh (2 Chr 33:12, 13), who for the Chronicler was a prototype of post-exilic Judah.

Hezekiah's reign reestablished the religious ideals associated with the reigns of David (2 Chr 29:2, 25–30) and Solomon (30:26). Josiah urged the Levites of his day to comply with ancient directions laid down by David and Solomon concerning their part in temple worship (35:4).

This presentation of the first two Davidic kings as models for Judah and its leaders in a post-exilic presentation of history is suggestive for the Psalter. Was this focus associated with a comparable interpretation of David as a model for individual piety? If so, much is achieved toward spanning the gap between ancient history and contemporary relevance. The ancient hero became a standard of spirituality for members of each generation of God's people, however hard times were and even when sin had triumphed. Not only the historicizing superscriptions but even the simple headings "psalm of David" would carry the message of a spiritual model from whom each hearer or reader was invited to learn.

3. *The editorial function of Ps 19.* Is there any evidence in the Psalter itself for a modeling focus upon David? The purpose of Ps 19 is worth considering in this respect.

Of itself it is a Torah-wisdom composition prefaced with a creation hymn. Contextually it interrupts a sequence of royal psalms, Pss 18, 20, and 21. The discussion of similar insertions in the first chapter encourages us to ask whether we can detect a positive intention in this case. In fact there is a remarkable overlap of terminology between Ps 18 and

19:7-14. Yahweh is hailed with the language of trust as "my rock" in 18:2, 46 and 19:14. His "judgments" or "ordinances" feature in 18:22 and 19:9. The attaining of human blamelessness is mentioned in 18:23, 25 and 19:13.

What is postulated of Yahweh in Ps 18 is in three cases applied to his Torah in Ps 19, in an inverted order. Yahweh shows himself pure (18:26), and his Torah is pure (19:9). Yahweh gives light (18:29), and so does his Torah (19:8). Yahweh's way is perfect (18:30), and so is his Torah (19:7). Moreover, in the superscription of Ps 18 David is described as Yahweh's servant, while in 19:11 the psalmist describes himself prayerfully as "your servant."

The accumulation of parallels leads to a clear conclusion: the purpose of setting the two psalms side by side was to relate David's experience to the individual pious believer who sought models for personal living from the "Torah" of the Psalms. The application carries further a process already evident within Ps 18: twice a connection is traced between David's spirituality and generalized teaching, in vv 20-24/25-27 and 28-29. In his relation with God David was an exemplar for "all who seek refuge in him" (v 30).

Ps 19 has been placed next to Ps 18 in order that its second half may develop these hints which explicitly present David as a role model. From this perspective David is no longer the servant of Yahweh only in his special role as partner in a royal covenant. Now the term does not elevate him above Israel, but paradoxically brings him down to the level of the Israelite, who was committed by the bonds of a wider covenant to serve the same God. The description of "presumptuous sins" as an overpowering force in 19:13 may have been viewed as a reinterpretation of David's military enemies, in terms of spiritual warfare. Overall, the editorial message is that for the pious student of Torah the psalms of David open up fresh vistas in teaching how to live for God.

The New Testament received the Psalms as part of the Jewish Scriptures. It is worth asking what messages the Christian ear first heard from this heritage. Only a brief answer is possible here, which can by no means do full justice to the evidence, since the Psalter was the part of the Writings which the New Testament enthusiastically took to its heart, just as in the rest of the Jewish canon Deuteronomy was the part of the Law it prized and the book of Isaiah was its favorite among the Prophets.

1. *Christ in the Psalms.* The Old Testament provided a theological substructure, to use C. H. Dodd's phrase, for the Christian faith.[26] It served to exegete the person and work of Jesus. There was a process of mutual interaction, for the Old Testament was understood as explaining the phenomenon of Jesus, while in turn this phenomenon explained the Old Testament. For the church all things became new. New light was cast upon everything, including the Old Testament. From this fresh perspective the Psalms had something else to say beyond their earlier messages.

In the Letter to the Hebrews Jesus is regarded as the archetypal lamenter who through his experience of salvation from death became an agent of salvation for others. See Heb 5:7–9 and compare Ps 22:24:

> He [God] has not hidden his face from him,
> but when he cried for help, he heard him.

Accordingly, as risen from the dead, Jesus became the archetypal giver of thanks:

> "I will proclaim thy name to my brethren,
> in the midst of the congregation I will praise thee."
> (Heb 2:12 RSV; Ps 22:22)

As heir to the royal psalms he is the king who is mysteriously associated with God in a metaphysical relationship:

"Thou art my son,
today I have begotten thee". . . . (1:5 RSV, 5:5; cf. Ps 2:7)
"Thy throne, O God, is for ever and ever,
the righteous scepter is the scepter of thy kingdom. . . ."
(1:8, 9 RSV; cf. Ps 45:6, 7)

He is the priest-king who has a sacrificial ministry:

"Thou art a priest for ever,
after the order of Melchizedek." (5:6 RSV; cf. Ps 110:4)

He has too a heavenly position of honor next to God, which guarantees the ultimate triumph of his cause:

"Sit at my right hand,
till I make thy enemies
a stool for thy feet". . . . (1:13 RSV; cf. Ps 110:1)

By a natural fusion of psalmodic and christological ideas he is also the king of creation:

"Thou, Lord, didst found the earth in the beginning, . . .
thou art the same,
and thy years will never end."
(1:10, 12 RSV; cf. Ps 102:25-27)

As archetypal representative of a new humanity, he has experienced in his own way the subordination and royal exaltation of Ps 8:4-6, made "'lower than the angels'" and "'crowned . . . with glory and honor'" (Heb 2:6-9 RSV). Once Jesus has come and done his work, a new understanding of Ps 40:6-8 leaps out at the reader: the verses serve to confirm the fact that Jesus has replaced a system of sacrifice with a new order based upon his own obedience to God, as Heb 10:5–10 explains. The hermeneutical interaction between the Psalter and the new revelation is a creative power that generates new praise to God.

Much of this reinterpretation of the Psalms is common to other parts of the New Testament. In particular Ps 22 with its contrasting pattern of suffering and triumph became an obvious quarry for christological parallels. In the Gospels the lamenting first half runs through the story of the cross. The initial verse received the honor of quotation on the lips of the dying Jesus:

> "My God, my God, why hast thou forsaken me?"
> (Matt 27:46 RSV; Mark 15:34)

Doubtless this solemn citation inspired further use of the psalm. Material from the lament section colored the terminology of the passion narrative and so conveyed a message that this tragedy was in accord with the divine will (see Matt 27:35, 39, 43; Mark 15:24, 29 and Luke 23:34, 35; compare Ps 22:7, 8, 18). The Fourth Gospel is more explicit: Ps 22 yielded a prophecy of the humiliation of Jesus:

> "They parted my garments among them,
> and for my clothing they cast lots."
> (John 19:24 RSV; Ps 22:18)

The beginning of the second half of Ps 22, v 22, resonant with God-given triumph, was not only cited in Heb 2:12 but also found an echo in the evangelists' narrative of the resurrection:

> "Do not hold me, for I have not ascended
>   to the Father, but
> go to my brethren and say to them, I am

ascending to my
Father and your Father, to my God and your God."
(John 20:17 RSV; cf. Matt 28:10)

2. *The Psalms and the Christian believer.* The christological dimension of the Psalter in the New Testament did not
displace a prizing of the Psalms for their perennial, pastoral
value. The force of 2 Tim 4:17 has been considered already, in
the sixth chapter. The Letter to the Hebrews quotes an affirmation of faith as still relevant for the writer and his readers:

"The Lord is my helper,
I will not be afraid,
what can man do to me?" (13:6 RSV; cf. Ps 118:6)

The prophetic warning of Ps 95:7–11, "'Today, when you
hear his voice, do not harden your hearts . . . ,'" rings out
again with contemporary urgency as the incisive, searching
word of God, "sharper than any two-edged sword, piercing
to the division of soul and spirit. . . ." (Heb 3:7; 4:12 RSV)

Similarly, in the Letter to the Romans the truth that the
Israelite community of faith had a hope in God which was not
disappointed (Ps 22:5) finds an echo in a comparable situation
of communal suffering (Rom 5:5). The solace of the psalms of
disorientation is demonstrated afresh in Rom 8:36. It cites the
self-descriptive element of a communal lament, Ps 44:22, and
relates it to Christian persecution and martyrdom:

"For thy sake we are being killed all the day long;
we are regarded as sheep to be slaughtered."
(Rom 8:36 RSV)

At first sight the reference is surprising and looks out of
place. Were not present sufferings insignificant in comparison with eternal glory (8:18)? Was not the love of Christ an

all-conquering power which took persecution and death in its triumphant stride (8:35, 38)? Yes indeed, but triumph is not triumphalism. The apostle was human enough to know that the sword, and fear of the sword, inflicted pain from which Christians are not yet immune (see vv 23, 26). Cries of anguish escape from Christian lips as readily as from Israelite lips. In pastoral vein Paul lingered on the pangs of disorientation, for which the noblest of causes is no anodyne. It is in accord with this pastoral note that mention of suffering is tenderly wrapped around with "the love of Christ" and "the love of God in Christ" (vv 35, 39).

For the New Testament writers the Psalter continues to preach the gospel of a God who cares; they pointed to Jesus as the loving mediator of this care. Prayer and praise, faith and hope still flowed from the human heart in living rapport with the Psalms. Voicing of them in lament and song now rise to God through the fitting agency of a Lord who represents God before humanity and humanity before God.

NOTES

1. *The Editing of the Hebrew Psalter* (Chico, Calif.: Scholars Press, 1985), pp. 139–197, esp. pp. 174–176.

2. Much of this work is locked up in German publications. English readers may refer to H. Gunkel, *The Psalms: A Form-critical Introduction* (Philadelphia: Fortress, 1967); S. Mowinckel, *The Psalms in Israel's Worship*, 2 vols. (New York: Abingdon, 1962); H. J. Kraus, *Theology of the Psalms* (Minneapolis: Augsburg, 1986); C. Westermann, *The Psalms: Structure, Content and Message* (Minneapolis: Augsburg, 1980); and *Praise and Lament in the Psalms* (Atlanta: John Knox, 1981).

3. *The Psalms in Israel's Worship*, vol. 1, pp. 1–12.

4. For this interpretation see P. C. Craigie, *Psalms 1–50* (Waco, Tex.: Word, 1983), pp. 236–241.

5. This interpretation, advocated by Kraus and others, has been followed by Craigie, *Psalms 1–50*, pp. 198–200.

6. This hermeneutical frame of reference is most easily accessible to the reader in Brueggemann's *The Message of the Psalms* (Minneapolis: Augsburg, 1984), pp. 9–11 and then *passim*.

7. *Commentary on the Book of Psalms*, vol. 1 (Grand Rapids: Eerdmans, reprinted, 1949), p. xxxvii.

8. *The Editing of the Hebrew Psalter*, pp. 188f.

9. See my *Psalms 101–150* (Waco, Tex.: Word, 1983), pp. 49–51 for elaboration.

10. See *Psalms 101–150*, pp. 60f., for discussion.

11. *Praise and Lament in the Psalms*, pp. 70–75.

12. *Psalms 1–50*, p. 73.

13. *The Editing of the Hebrew Psalter*, pp. 164, 190.

14. See my *Psalms 101–150*, pp. 9, 160. This insight relies on the research of K. W. Neubauer in his Berlin dissertation of 1964.

15. C. Westermann has emphasized the role of blessing in the Old Testament in *Elements of Old Testament Theology* (Atlanta: John Knox, 1982), pp. 85–117.

16. *Psalms 1–50*, p. 92.

17. *Psalms 1–50*, p. 163.

18. See K. D. Sakenfeld, *Faithfulness in Action* (Philadelphia: Fortress, 1985), pp. 83–100. A more detailed treatment may be found in her *The Meaning of Hesed in the Hebrew Bible* (Missoula, Mont.: Scholars Press, 1978), pp. 215–231.

19. *The Book of Psalms* (London: Oliphants, 1972), vol. 1, p. 512.

20. G. von Rad, *Old Testament Theology*, vol. 2 (London: SCM Press, 1979), p. 319.

21. *Praise and Lament in the Psalms*, pp. 257f.

22. *Praise and Lament in the Psalms*, p. 253.

23. *Introduction to the Old Testament as Scripture* (Philadelphia: John Knox, 1979), p. 513; cf. Westermann, *Praise and Lament in the Psalms*, p. 253.

24. *Introduction to the OT as Scripture*, p. 521.

25. See my *Psalms 101–150*, pp. 278f., with reference to the work of E. Slomovic and others.

26. The subtitle of his book *According to the Scriptures* (London: Nisbet, 1952) was *The Substructure of New Testament Theology*.

SELECT BIBLIOGRAPHY

Allen, L. C. *Psalms 101–150*. Word Biblical Commentary. Waco, Tex.: Word Books, 1983.

Anderson, A. A. *The Book of Psalms*. 2 vols, The New Century Bible. London: Oliphants, 1972.

Anderson, B. W. *Out of the Depths: The Psalms Speak for Us Today*. revised ed. Philadelphia: Westminster Press, 1983.

Bonhoeffer, D. *Psalms: The Prayerbook of the Bible*. tr. J. H. Burtness. Minneapolis: Augsburg Publishing House, 1970.

Brueggemann, W. *The Message of the Psalms: A Theological Commentary*. Augsburg Old Testament Studies. Minneapolis: Augsburg Publishing House, 1984.

Childs, B. S. *Introduction to the Old Testament as Scripture*. Philadelphia: Westminster Press, 1980.

Craigie, P. C. *Psalms 1–50*. Word Biblical Commentary. Waco, Tex.: Word Books, 1983.

Gunn, G. S. *God in the Psalms*. Edinburgh: Saint Andrew Press, 1956.

Guthrie, H. H. *Israel's Sacred Psalms: A Study of Dominant Themes*. New York: Seabury Press, 1966.

Johnson, A. R. *The Cultic Prophet and Israel's Psalmody*. Cardiff: University of Wales Press, 1962.

Miller, Jr., P. D. *Interpreting the Psalms*. Philadelphia: Fortress Press, 1986.

Weiser, A. *The Psalms: A Commentary*. tr. H. Hartwell. Old Testament Library. Philadelphia: Westminster Press, 1962.

Westermann, C. *The Psalms: Structure, Content and Message*. tr. R. D. Gehrke. Minneapolis: Augsburg Publishing House, 1980.

———. *Praise and Lament in the Psalms*. tr. K. R. Crim and R. N. Soulen. Edinburgh: T. & T. Clark, 1981.

Wilson, G. H. *The Editing of the Hebrew Psalter*. Society of Biblical Literature Dissertation Series. Chico, Calif.: Scholars Press, 1985.

INDEX OF PSALMS CITED

22	70, 71, 88	29		79	39	94
22:1	52, 60, 128	29:11		84	39:7	106
22:2	71					
22:3-5	60, 98	30		20		
22:3	55	30:1-5		38	40:1-2	109
22:4	71	30:1-3		21	40:3	110
22:5	129	30:3		90	40:4	72
22:7-8	128	30:4-5		21, 51	40:6-8	127
22:10	61, 97	30:6-7		21, 38	41:13	13
22:12	89	30:7-10		38	42-64	55
22:13	89	30:8-11		21	42-49	14
22:15	92	30:9		58	42	16
22:16	89	30:11-12		38	42:5	107
22:18	128	30:11		29	42:11	107
22:20-21	90	30:12		21, 39	43:2-3	60
22:21	28, 88	31:4		89	42:5	107
22:22	126, 128	31:5		62	44	19
22:23-31	28	31:6		62, 70	44:1-3	53, 98
22:23-24	50	31:7-8		89	44:4	62
22:24	126	31:14		62	44:6-8	61
22:25	43	31:16		62	44:6	70
22:26	29, 109	31:24		109	44:17-21	97
23	20, 25	32		32, 91, 94	44:17-18	60
23:1-4	63	32:6		95	44:22	129
23:1-3	64	32:10-11		16	44:26	97
23:1	64	32:11		50	45	14
23:4-5	64	33		16	45:6-7	117, 127
23:5-6	64	33:1-3		29	46	22, 69
23:6	64	33:1		16	46:1	68
24	29	33:5		16, 78, 103	46:5	35, 68
24:3-6	119	33:16		70	46:7	68
24:3	80	33:18-19		107	46:8-10	68
24:5	80	33:18		16, 101, 103	46:11	68
25	94	33:20		101	48	22
25:5	107	33:22		16, 103	48:3-7	68
25:6	94	34		32, 123	48:9	105
25:11	95	34:8		72	48:14	105
25:15	89	35:24		95	49	31
25:17	89	36:5-9		55	49:6	70
25:20-21	101	36:7-9		31		
27:1	63, 90	37		31, 56	50	14, 16
27:3	63	37:3		70, 111	50:8-15	16
27:7-12	65	37:9		111	50:23	16
27:13	65	37:11		111	51-71	16
27:14	108	37:22		111	51	91, 123
28:2	66	37:29		111	51:16-19	16
28:5	28	37:34		111	52	123
28:6-7	66	38		94	52:7	70
28:6	28	38:1-5		94	54	122
28:9	40	38:15		108	54:3	68

137

Index

PSALMS

Leslie C. Allen

Leslie C. Allen is Professor of Old Testament at Fuller Theological Seminary. Formerly he was Lecturer in Hebrew, Aramaic, and Judaism at London Bible College for more than twenty years. He holds the M.A. degree from Corpus Christi College, Cambridge, in Classics and Oriental Studies. His Ph.D. is from the University College of London, in Hebrew. Among his publications are *The Greek Chronicles Parts 1 and 2 and The Books of Joel, Obadiah, Jonah, and Micah* for The New International Commentary on the Old Testament, as well as the section on Psalms 73-150, in *A Bible Commentary for Today* edited by Howley, Bruce, and Ellison.